Classics in Sequence

*A source book for
MIDI sequencing*

William Lloyd *and* **Paul Terry**

● Musonix Publishing ●

*To Alfie Lloyd, John Robertson and Sue Gohren
and for Graeme White, who started the ball rolling*

Other titles from Musonix:

Music in Sequence – A complete guide to MIDI sequencing
Rock in Sequence – An anthology of hits for sequencing *
The Studio Musician's Jargonbuster – A glossary of music technology and recording
Rehearse, Direct and Play – A student's guide to group music making

* Available late 1995 in the UK and Australia only

First published in 1992
Reprinted with revisions, 1995   ISBN Number   0 9517214 1 0

Published by Musonix Publishing, 2 Avenue Gardens, London SW14 8BP.

Exclusive distributors:	Music Sales Limited	Music Sales Corporation	Music Sales Pty. Limited
	8/9 Frith Street	257 Park Avenue South	120 Rothschild Avenue
	London W1V 5TZ	New York NY 10010 USA	Rosebery NSW 2018 Australia

Cover design by Bob Linney

Excerpt from Præludium and Allegro in the style of Pugnani by Fritz Kreisler,
© 1910 B. Schott's Söhne, Mainz. Reprinted by permission of Schott & Co. Ltd., London.

Excerpt from La Fille Mal Gardée by Hérold / Lanchbery,
© 1960 Oxford University Press. Reprinted by permission.

Tanz from Carmina Burana by Carl Orff,
© 1937 B. Schott's Söhne, Mainz. Reprinted by permission of Schott & Co. Ltd., London.

Excerpt from Piano Phase by Steve Reich,
© 1980 Universal Edition (London) Ltd. Reprinted by permission – all rights reserved.

Typeset in 11-point Times Roman on Xerox Ventura Publisher™,
with music processed in Score™ from Passport Designs, Inc.

Printed and bound in England.

Contents

Introduction

You may be surprised to find a book devoted to the sequencing of classical music. Many people tend to associate the classics with the rather stuffy world of the concert hall and opera house, and sequencers with the hi-tech glitz of the rock studio. However, since all styles of music are constructed from the same basic components, such subjective judgements are meaningless in purely technological terms.

A sequence is a series of events that follow each other in order. The term **sequencer** was first coined in the early seventies, when the burgeoning electronics industry produced a device that was capable of storing sufficient data to enable a handful of notes to be repeated automatically on a synthesizer. Any aid that could, however modestly, help the musician use the astonishingly complex early synths was destined to succeed.

The increasing popularity of sequencers also brought with it problems, as there was no universal system for connecting them to synths and other equipment. Thus there was no certainty that a sequencer would work correctly, or even at all, with any synth other than the one for which it was designed.

Recognizing this problem, a group of manufacturers agreed on a standard in 1983 that would allow any electronic musical instrument suitably equipped to communicate, or interface, with another. This was called MIDI (Musical Instrument Digital Interface) and is still, essentially, the system in use today.

Sequencers developed rapidly from their humble origins and can now store and manipulate with ease the mass of data needed for long and complex compositions. Combined with a modern synth producing sounds of almost infinite subtlety, it is now possible for the single musician to create and control every aspect of a full ensemble piece in almost any musical style.

A book of classics for sequencing would have seemed a nonsense only ten years ago. Now we are able to present such a collection in the knowledge that you will enjoy creating your own unique performances of the pieces and with the hope that the very act of sequencing will lead you, as it has led us, to a greater understanding of the music itself.

We have chosen music which, while possibly being familiar, is not always easy to obtain in printed form. We do not claim the pieces to be uniquely representative of the work of their composers or periods as they have been chosen primarily for their suitability for sequencing. The sophistication of the modern sequencer is not yet limitless, though, and thus the regular rhythms of the dance have a prominent place here, while the elegant phrasing of classical music, the fleeting nuances of romantic music and the exciting complexities of modern scores may appear too rarely for some tastes – although later chapters deal with some of these challenges.

If you are new to sequencing, we recommend first working through our companion volume, ***Music in Sequence***, which deals with some of the basic note-reading and sequencing skills needed in a wide variety of musical styles. As in that book, our aim here is not to present yet another technical manual, but to explain how to interpret music using the technology creatively. We hope you enjoy it.

William Lloyd and Paul Terry

The Sequencing Studio

THE BASIC SYSTEM

Sequencers come as software programs for computers and as hardware units that are either free-standing or built into a **synthesizer**. Hardware sequencers are robust and easily transportable, making them suitable for live playback work, but recording and editing can be difficult as they generally have tiny display panels and limited editing facilities. A **computer-based** system is a more expensive option, but it provides a full-screen display, a larger memory for sequences and easier operation with the computer's mouse and keyboard. Software can be upgraded when new products appear, and the computer can also be used for many other musical and non-musical tasks.

The best type of synthesizer to use for sequencing is **multi-timbral** – one which can play a number of different sounds (**voices**) simultaneously. Synth specifications will state the maximum number of multi-timbral voices, often 8 or 16. Don't confuse this with the figure quoted for the synth's *polyphony*, usually 16 or 32, which simply refers to the maximum number of *notes* that can sound together. The total number of voices available on the synth will be much greater than either of these – 64, 128 or more.

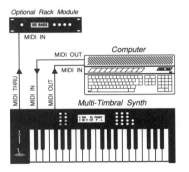

Unless your sequencer is built into the synth, you will need to connect the two with **MIDI leads**. The MIDI OUT from the synth sends electronic data about your playing to the sequencer for recording, while the sequencer's MIDI OUT relays the recorded signals back to the synth for performance *(see left)*. If you do not wish to work with **headphones**, you will also need a **powered monitor** in order to hear the music. In this context, monitor is another word for a robust loudspeaker: "powered" refers to the fact that it contains its own amplifier. Two of them will be needed for stereo sound. Using a hi-fi amplifier and speakers is not a good idea, as they can easily be damaged by the wide output range of a synth.

EXPANSION

Many users soon feel the need to extend their sound-generating facilities. This can be done simply by adding a **rack module** or **expander** – a sound generator without a keyboard that is controlled from your main synth. For sequencing it can be connected to the system as shown in the diagram – the MIDI THRU socket merely duplicates the data being sent from the sequencer. A particularly useful expander for sequencing classical music is a multi-timbral orchestral **sample player**. Samples are digital recordings of individual notes played on live instruments which can be triggered from your keyboard: they can sound more realistic than even the best synthesized versions.

A **reverberation** (or multi-effects) unit will add a professional touch to the finished sequence. These are often built into synth **workstations**. Separate units can be controlled from the sequencer if they have a MIDI interface, thus allowing you to trigger the correct reverb settings for each piece you sequence.

RECORDING

You will probably want to record your work. If you use just a single synth you can connect its line outputs directly to an ordinary **stereo cassette recorder**. However, handling multiple outputs will really need a basic mixing desk. A four or eight-track "portastudio" can be used for this, although multi-track recording will only be needed if you want to add live musicians – and you will still have to produce a two-track tape at the end of the day. The mixing and balancing of the synth tracks is, in any case, best done from the sequencer.

MIDI MESSAGES

MIDI allows basic performance instructions, such as the pitch and loudness of notes, to be transmitted between pieces of compatible equipment *via* a MIDI lead. A lot of information can be sent very quickly: up to 31,250 signals per second, in fact. These binary pulses are grouped to form meaningful messages, such as "Note On" – the instruction to start playing a note.

The MIDI Note On message actually consists of three parts: a "status byte" which tells the synth that the command is to turn a note on, followed by two data bytes – detailing the pitch of the note and its loudness.

Clearly, the system also needs to know which synth, or which voice within a multi-timbral synth, is to play this note. For this purpose, the status byte also includes a **channel number** between 1 and 16. Only instruments in the system set to receive on that channel will respond. A multi-timbral synth behaves like a group of synths: it can listen to a number of channels simultaneously and can play each on a different voice.

The limitation of MIDI to 16 channels can be a problem if you have the capacity to use more than 16 voices at once. A MIDI split box will not help – it gives extra sockets but not extra channels. However, special MIDI interfaces are available which provide 64 channels or more, separated into groups of 16, with each set going through a separate MIDI port and cable to the relevant synth. They are not cheap, however, and you can normally only use such a device with the particular sequencer program for which it is intended.

MIDI is a serial system: it can deal with only one message at a time. In a chord the notes are actually played one after the other in very quick succession, although the ear is deceived by the speed of MIDI into hearing perfectly synchronized notes:

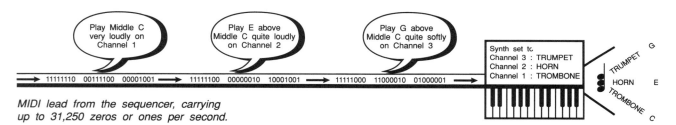

MIDI lead from the sequencer, carrying up to 31,250 zeros or ones per second.

Much more goes on than we can show in the simple diagram *above*. Every Note On must be followed by a Note Off message, the time between the two dictating the actual note length. MIDI also deals with other types of messages – for changing voices or operating controllers such as modulation wheels and foot pedals. It is even possible to transmit the entire structure of a freshly edited synth voice by means of a SysEx (Systems Exclusive) message.

Some actions, such as using aftertouch (pushing hard into a key after the start of a note) can generate huge quantities of MIDI data. In complex pieces it is possible to overload the system, causing "MIDI choke". More common, though, are problems caused by overloading the synth rather than MIDI – asking for 17 simultaneous notes on a synth with 16-note polyphony, for example, will cut off the first note of the chord when the 17th note arrives.

Almost all the data needed to create the finest performance is encapsulated within the simple framework of MIDI. The manipulation of this digital information, whether the subtle adjustment of note lengths required to shape musical phrases, the sudden loudness of an accent or the tapered volume levels of a *crescendo,* is where you and the sequencer come in.

Setting up the synthesizer

Setting-up a synth for sequencing takes a little time, but should be a once-only procedure, as the settings can be saved in the synth's memory for future use.

In order to receive data on several MIDI channels at the same time, the synth must be in Multi-Timbral (sometimes called Combi) mode and a patch or combination must be selected that can receive on several MIDI channels at once. Although some synths offer many such configurations, only one is needed for all your sequencing, and this should be as uncluttered as possible. If your synth does not offer a suitable preset, create your own as follows:

1. Find an existing combination that you don't mind altering.

2. Assign a different MIDI channel to each of the instruments within the patch. You will probably find it simplest to use consecutive channel numbers: perhaps 1-8 on your main synth, leaving 9-16 for a second synth or expander if you have one.

3. Select a clear voice for each channel. It is unimportant precisely which sounds you choose, as each sequence can reset this part of the combination. You may care to set a group of standard sounds ready for use with the music in this book, such as Flute, Oboe, Trumpet, Strings, Bass and Piano.

4. Make sure that each instrument is set to be available at maximum output level, with no transposition in operation, and able to operate over the entire pitch range (*ie* not limited by a pitch "window").

5. Each voice should have MIDI program change, controller and aftertouch enabled (filters off) as these are features required by sequences in this book.

6. Functions such as detuning (thickening of sound) and effects (*eg* reverb) can be set for each voice as desired. Some panning of channels to left and right will give a rough impression of stereo space – more specific placing can be achieved from the sequencer.

7. Re-name the combination and save it in your synth's internal memory.

Setting Instrument 3 to Channel 4, voiced for Oboe 23, in a multi-timbral combination. The sound is Panned left and has its output Level set to the maximum 99.

Your synth manual should show you how to do all this and how to save the settings. Then you only need to turn the equipment on at the start of a session and select your sequencing patch on the synth in order to start.

GLOBAL CHANNEL

Some synths use one channel (known sometimes as the global or common channel) for certain operations which affect the instrument as a whole. This is usually MIDI channel 1, although it can be reassigned. A voice number set on the sequencer for the global channel *may* throw the synth into entirely the wrong combination. There is no quick solution to this problem and (if it affects your system) it is probably easiest to change the global channel to 16 and then avoid using it in your sequences.

While the synth has been set to listen to a number of channels simultaneously, it normally only transmits on one channel at a time (usually the global channel). So, even though you may hear the flute sound that you assigned to, say, channel 2, during playback, the synth may annoyingly produce a quite different voice as you record:

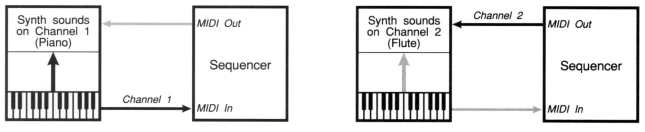

A piano sound is heard when recording   *A flute sound is heard on playback*

This is not ideal: it is much better to record using the right voice, as you can then match your playing style to the characteristics of the sound you want.

**LOCAL OFF &
MIDI THRU**

To get round this problem, most synths allow you to sever the connection between the keyboard and sound generator by setting a switch in the synth called **Local** to off. The signal then goes only to your sequencer, in which another switch called **MIDI Thru** immediately echoes the data back to the synth along the return MIDI lead, but now on channel 2 so that the intended flute voice is heard while you play:

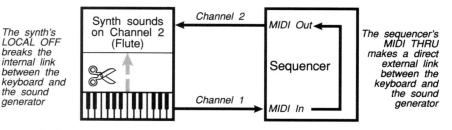

A flute sound is now heard on both recording and playback

If you use this MIDI Thru facility it is important to switch Local off in the synth, otherwise every note will be played twice – once directly through the local connection, and again upon being echoed back from the sequencer. Even if you don't notice the double notes, they will quickly eat up your synth's polyphony and notes will thus start to disappear from thick textures.

The MIDI Thru facility is also needed if your system consists of a master keyboard (which has no sound generator of its own) and a separate rack module. You don't need to worry about Local off, of course, because the keyboard and sound generator are not connected except by MIDI.

Using The Sequencer

*This guide gives an overview of useful sequencer functions. The names and appearance of some features may be a little different on your own sequencer, but it will probably have most of the facilities listed here. Practical uses for many of these features will be found throughout this book, and its companion, **Music in Sequence**.*

TRACKS AND PARTS

When music is recorded into a sequencer it is stored as a series of **tracks**. These are the horizontal layers of your music and most sequencers allow you to divide them into shorter sections called **parts**:

	Bar Numbers	1	5	9	13	17
Track 1	Flute Solo			Verse		Chorus
Track 2	Piano Right Hand		Intro	Verse		Chorus
Track 3	Piano Left Hand		Intro	Verse		Chorus

In this example, there are three tracks: the identifying labels, like *Flute Solo,* can be typed in by the user. Similarly, each part (or pattern) can usually be given a name, such as *Intro,* to show its position in the music. Sequencers often allow you to **group** several parts or tracks together, so that they can be moved and worked on as a single unit.

The complete set-up of parts, tracks and instrumental voices that you choose to assign to those tracks is generally known as the **arrangement**.

Each individual instrumental line is normally recorded onto a different track. Sequencers offer more empty tracks than you will ever use, so don't be afraid to separate the strands of complex music, such as the treble and bass staves of piano music, and put them onto different tracks.

MIDI CHANNELS & VOICE NUMBERS

Typing names into a track or part, may be helpful to you but it is pretty meaningless to the synth that will play your music. In order for each track to use a different sound, it will have to be given a different MIDI channel number. If you want it to play on a voice other than the one already assigned to this channel in the synth, you will also need to set the voice number you require.

For example, if you set Track 2 to Channel 7 on the sequencer, and assign voice 23 to it, the synth will play the music using voice 23 – providing its multi-timbral patch is set to receive on Channel 7. Any voice already allocated on the synth will be over-ridden by the sequencer, unless either has been set to filter out voice changes (also called **program** changes). If your sequencer starts counting voices from 1 while the synth counts them from 0 you will always need to add one when making program changes in the sequence.

TRANSPORT CONTROLS

Most sequencers use icons that look like the controls of a cassette recorder for functions such as play, record, stop *etc*. Certain keys on the computer keyboard can be used to perform the same operations – the manual will give details of these. Keys which take you to the beginning of the sequence, or which start and stop playback are particularly handy, especially for those who dislike using a mouse. It is also possible for some sequencers to assign notes on the synth for triggering such functions remotely *via* MIDI.

●	■	>
Record	Stop	Play

≪	004 : 3 : 096	≫
	Bars Beats Ticks	
Rewind	SONG POINTER	Forward

Of course, you also need to know where you are in the music, and for this the sequencer's equivalent of the tape counter is the **song pointer** (bar counter). This shows the bar and beat number, together with the exact position within that beat. This is usually expressed as a number of ticks, with a quarter note typically divided into 192 ticks – although some sequencers can offer even higher resolution. The example *left,* shows a song position of bar 4, beat 3½.

00 : 00 : 16 : 12
SMPTE

Hours : Mins : Secs : Frames

5 : 1 : 000	8 : 1 : 000
Left Locator	Right Locator

Many sequencers also have a SMPTE counter (the acronym stands for Society of Motion Picture and Television Engineers). SMPTE is used to synchronize sound with film or video pictures, but is also useful for showing how far into a sequence you are in time *(see left)*. The frame refers to a single still picture on conventional film. Frame rates can be adjusted between 24 and 30 per second, depending on the synchronization system required.

Two other counters often found are the **left and right locators**. These enable you to isolate a specific part of your music (say, bar 5 to the start of bar 8) to be used for a particular operation, such as making a **loop** (cycle) for playback or perhaps for recording in just these specific bars.

Recording

TEMPO & TIME SIGNATURES

One of the advantages that the sequencer has over a standard tape recorder is its ability to play music at any speed (**tempo**) without affecting the pitch. A recording can therefore be made at whatever pace is comfortable and yet still be played back at the correct tempo. It is even possible to record notes one at a time *(see* step time *below)*.

Tempo is measured in beats per minute (**bpm**) and can be set in a range from 16 to 240 bpm or more. Because the sequencer organizes its information in bars and beats, you will also need to set a **time signature** indicating the number of beats per bar.

Bar	Time	Tempo
01:01:000	4/4	
01:01:000		120 bpm
25:01:000	3/4	
25:01:000		72 bpm

Using a Mastertrack to change to a slow triple time at bar 25

Sequencers handle alterations of speed later in the piece in a variety of ways. Some will take any changes you make in the tempo indicator and register them as special commands (sometimes called *pseudo events*) in the track, alongside the MIDI data. Others require you to enter this information manually into a special **tempo mastertrack**. You may also have to use this method for making any changes of time signature, if your sequencer does not automatically pick these up from the main screen *(see left)*.

To keep you in time when recording, each beat is sounded by the **metronome**. This can be output either as a beep from the computer or as a MIDI "click" which can sound any note on any channel you select. A **pre-count** (lead-in) of one or two bars will enable you to hear the tempo before recording starts.

RECORDING OPTIONS

The start point of a recording is usually set by entering a bar number in the left locator box or by positioning a cursor on the screen. Sometimes you will want to record a section in the middle of a track without affecting existing material on either side of it. This is called **punch-in** recording and will need to have start and end (**punch-out**) positions set in the locator boxes.

Sequencers generally offer two recording modes. **Replace** will, like a tape recorder, erase any existing material on the track. **Overdub**, on the other hand, will add new material without deleting anything already recorded. This is very useful if you want to input complex or chordal music one line at a time.

It is not necessary to record music in **real time** – that is, played in rhythm, however slowly. Notes can be entered in **step time**, where you specify the type of note length required, and then play at leisure without the need to keep to a regular metronome beat. Fast-moving music can be recorded easily and accurately with this method and it is particularly useful when there are many notes of the same length to record.

Finally, although we have assumed that most users will record their sequences from a keyboard, other options for input are available – such as MIDI guitar and wind controllers – which non-keyboard players may prefer.

NOTE EDITING

Most sequencers offer several ways of viewing and editing notes and other MIDI information in a part or track:

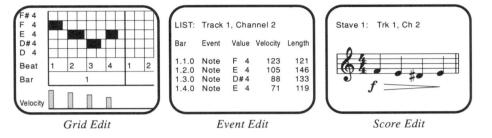

Grid Edit　　　　　*Event Edit*　　　　　*Score Edit*

The graphic display of a **grid edit** shows the pitch, position and length of each note, any of which can be altered using the computer's mouse. Additional information, such as individual **velocity** (loudness) levels, can be called up and adjusted and notes may be copied, moved or erased.

The **event edit** (or list edit) system deals largely in numbers and is useful for really fine adjustments to data. It is the place to look if something untoward is happening for which no other explanation is immediately apparent. The **score edit**, impressive as it looks, is the least useful platform for editing, as music notation cannot reflect the finer rhythmic details of performance. Its main function is for preparing sequenced material for printing out.

GROUP EDITING

With any of these methods it is usually possible to highlight a group of notes for mass editing. However, the screen size restricts the amount of data that can be shown, so sequencers offer a range of group editing facilities for entire tracks, patterns or bar-ranges. Some of these, such as **delete**, **copy** and **move**, are clear in meaning but the purpose of others may not be so obvious.

PITCH

Transpose moves the pitch of all notes up or down by a number of semitones. This will put the music into a new key. Some sequencers provide more complex options such as **harmonic transpose** which also shifts patterns up or down, but makes further individual pitch adjustments to keep the music true to its original key signature.

VELOCITY

Velocity transformations adjust the loudness (dynamics) of notes. **Set velocity** will make all notes boringly equal in volume at whatever level you request. **Adjust velocity** will add to (or subtract from) the existing levels of each note, leaving the original contours of the pattern intact. A **crescendo** transform will ramp velocity levels across a range of notes to make gradual dynamic changes.

RHYTHM

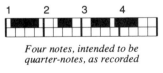

Four notes, intended to be quarter-notes, as recorded

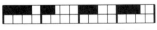

Quantizing to quarters locks them to the nearest quarter-note beats

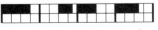

Quantizing to eighths pushes the second note to the wrong position

Imprecise rhythms can be nudged into place by **quantization**. This moves any rogue notes onto the nearest unit you specify – such as a sixteenth note (16), eighth (8), quarter (4), *etc*. Sequencers also provide for the temporary division of the beat into threes with a selection of triplet quantize values – 8T (or 12), 16T (or 24) and so on.

TIP There are two rules for successful quantization: (1) the quantize value must not be greater than the shortest type of note in the music you are processing, otherwise these will get merged with their neighbours; (2) none of the original recording must be out of time by more than 50% of the quantize value, or any such notes will get pushed onto the wrong beats. Most programs load with a default quantize value of 16 – make sure you change it if necessary!

Locking notes ruthlessly onto their correct beats can make some music sound unsuitably robotic. If this proves hard to undo, a **humanize** option will attempt to restore the feel of a live performance by randomly moving notes slightly

Four notes after normal quantization of note starts

A fixed length quantize to eighths makes all notes the same length

A legato quantize removes any gaps between notes

out of position – the reverse of quantizing, in fact. The problem can be avoided in the first place by using a **percentage quantize**: a 50% setting, for example, will move notes just halfway towards their correct places.

A **note length** (or duration) quantize will make note lengths an exact multiple of the set value without affecting their starting positions. **Fixed length** (or Set Duration) quantizing makes all notes the same length. Many sequencers offer a **legato** option which lengthens notes in order to close any gaps between them: it will not adjust overlapping notes, though. Finally, if you have produced a particularly good instinctive rhythm pattern, a **match** or **groove** quantize may allow you to line other parts up with it.

TIP You may find a facility called **auto quantize**. This will quantize your playing as you record – instantly obliterating any rhythmic subtlety before you have had a chance to listen back: avoid it like the plague!

Playback options

Sequencers offer many features designed to help you audition your work. These are often found on the "front page" (main screen) or in a track information box. It is usually possible to **solo**, **mute**, **loop**, **quantize** or **transpose** tracks. There may also be options to adjust track **velocity** levels and to **delay** (or advance) the output of one track in relation to the others. Most useful are the facilities to set a track's **program** number, **pan** position and **output volume** level. You can thus try a track on a variety of voices at different levels and positions in the mix.

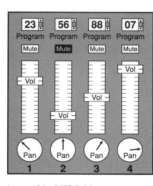

A graphic MIDI Mixer screen on the sequencer offers a particularly easy way of controlling playback settings for each track in the mix.

These front page functions are designed to be "non-destructive" – they modify the MIDI output while leaving the original data in the sequence intact, making it possible to experiment with different values while the music is playing. Thus, a track transposed on the front page will still appear in its original key on the edit screens. Some sequencers provide graphic **MIDI mixers** for easy manipulation of playback data, enabling you to control the performance of your sequence from a single screen and store the settings for future use.

Editing MIDI

MIDI CONTROLLERS

In addition to recording and editing basic note information, you will almost certainly need to work with other MIDI instructions for controlling the synth. MIDI includes **controller** messages, such as modulation, pan and volume, and **channel** messages such as program change, pitch bend and aftertouch. Data for many of these can be recorded by the sequencer as you operate the synth's various controls, or it can be step-written directly into the sequence.

LIST:	Track 1, Channel 2		
Bar	Event	Val. 1	Val. 2	Value 3
1.1.0	Note	F 4 123	121
1.2.0	Note	E 4 105	146
1.3.0	Note	D#4 88	133
1.4.0	Note	E 4 71	119
1.4.48	Prog	23 --	Oboe
1.4.96	Contrl	10 127	Pan
2.1.0	Note	F 4 84	63
2.2.0	Note	E 4 78	67
2.3.0	Note	F 4 87	66
2.4.0	Contrl	7 120	Volume
3.1.0	Note	F 4 81	118
3.1.0	P_User	1 72	Tempo
3.2.0	Note	F#4 77	116
3.2.96	Note	G 4 79	109

MIDI data on an Event Edit list can be added, changed or deleted. A controller message for panning the channel to 127 is selected, to place the oboe voice on the far right.

Individual MIDI events are usually edited alongside note information on the edit screens *(see left)*, although they will not necessarily be displayed unless specially requested. Note that most synths implement only a selection of the wide range of control messages that are offered by sequencers.

While simple sequences may require little of this type of MIDI editing, familiarity with the procedures will be essential for sequencers with limited front-page settings or those which will not otherwise let you change program in mid track. It is also necessary for MIDI data to be written permanently into the sequence if you want to save your work as a standard MIDI file *(see below)* since this format ignores most front-page settings – an option such as **freeze play parameters** may be available to transfer these settings for you.

SAVING AND LOADING

Files
Save
Save As . .
Load
Delete
Quit

Save As . . .
Song
Track
Arrangement
Drum Map
MIDI File

A **files** menu will contain various options for saving and loading your work. Every manufacturer uses a different format for saving sequences to disk, thus ensuring that work saved in one sequencer will not load into one of a different make. A way around this annoying problem is mentioned *below*.

When saving a file, you should choose a name that will identify the contents for future reference: something like BACHARIA perhaps (many systems limit the name to eight characters). Sequences are normally saved as a **song file**, as this type will store all the musical data you have recorded. Many programs add a three-letter extension to the name, such as .SNG, .SON or .ALL.

It is usually possible to save selected parts of a recording, perhaps for merging into other pieces. An individual track (a bass part, for example) might be saved in a **track file**. A particular set-up of tracks, voices and other settings could be stored as an **arrangement** to form a template for other sequences, or the note numbers needed to trigger the instruments of a specific drum kit voice might be saved as a **drum map**.

Most sequencers give you this sort of variety when you select **load** (or open) to retrieve your work from disk and when you use the **save as...** function. Subsequently, you can use plain **save**, which will continue to store work with the name, and in the format, you have already chosen. To conserve disk space, check that you do not save unnecessary detail, such as any unwanted MIDI aftertouch data or even redundant sequences lurking in hidden windows.

TIP **Autosave** is a feature that will save files automatically at certain preset intervals. You may find, however, that the advantages of this are more than offset when autosave promptly preserves for posterity your latest and most mangled edit of a sequence, over-writing any more salvagable versions in the process. Much more useful is a facility to make **backup** versions of your files.

One final type of file, designed to get round the incompatibility problems of other formats, is the **MIDI file**. This basic file standard can be accepted by most sequencers, providing the computer's operating system can read the actual disk. This will allow your data to be played through other makes of sequencer, but remember that only track information is stored – most "front page" settings will be ignored. If given a choice, use a Type 1 MIDI file, since Type 0 puts all the data onto one track and Type 2 is often not implemented.

GENERAL MIDI

Even if you succeed in transferring a sequence using a MIDI file, the program numbers you set for your own synth will probably trigger the wrong voices on a different instrument. Manufacturers are addressing the problem with a system called **General MIDI**. This includes a standard list of 128 useful sounds, to which all their instruments will conform, meaning that voice 1 will always be a piano, voice 57 a trumpet, *etc*. The intention is that voiced sequences will be roughly recognizable on any synth.

DISK ROUTINE

One of the most annoying and common occurrences is to lose valuable work that should be safe on disk. The following points will help avoid this danger:

1. Save your work to disk *frequently* and keep back-ups of everything.
2. Never allow anyone to use a disk in your equipment unless you know its origins and are certain that it is free of any computer virus.
3. Have spare formatted disks ready to use when the current working disk is full: you can't always format new disks once a program is loaded.
4. Prevent accidental erasure by using the "write protect" notch on disks.
5. Label disks clearly and store them away from equipment that generates magnetic fields, such as loudspeakers.

The sequencer program disk needs special care. Always make a copy and work from that, not the original. Unless your particular program requires access to the disk while operating, remove it from the disk drive as soon as it has loaded. If your program requires a security "dongle", never insert or remove it while the computer is switched on.

The music in this book

We have organized this book so that more complex aspects of sequencing and playing are left until later: you will see that this has led to the music being presented largely in chronological order. Some of the sequences are extracts from larger works, although we have tried always to reproduce the composer's intentions and to provide music that will be satisfying as it stands.

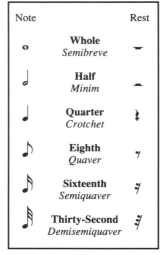

Original instrumentation has been indicated, together with hints on how to make a realistic voicing: other sounds may suggest themselves as you work on the pieces. We have occasionally slightly simplified the music to make it easier to record, including printing parts for transposing instruments at their correct sounding pitch.

We have described Middle C as C4 in this book, although some equipment annoyingly refers to it as C3. Octave differences can also be a problem with certain bass voices. Some of these sound an octave lower than their position on the keyboard would suggest – you may need to take this into account when recording bass parts. Note lengths are given as proportions of a whole note – readers used to the traditional English names may find the table *left* useful.

Sections devoted to music notation or keyboard technique have not been included since plenty of information on these topics is available elsewhere. Those new to sequencing will find plenty of basic help in ***Music in Sequence.***

Developments

MUSIC RESOURCES

At the end of many chapters we have included a list of additional pieces that will sequence well. The scores should be obtainable from your local library or music store. Music technology retailers often do not sell printed music and even music stores may not carry a large stock, although they should be able to order specific items and some offer a mail order service by telephone.

Piano music and songs are usually collected into **albums** of works by a single composer or pieces which share a theme, such as Broadway musicals. Popular numbers are sometimes available separately as **sheet music**.

Orchestral pieces are most easily obtained as **miniature scores** which display each instrumental part on a separate stave, as shown on page 72. Although the print is very small, these are preferable to piano arrangements which omit detail and give no indication of the original layout. Operas usually come as **vocal scores**, with the orchestral parts arranged for piano, although libraries may have full scores.

Whatever type of score is used, some arranging for sequencing will be needed. This includes identifying melodies, bass lines and accompaniments, looking out for copyable patterns and, particularly in orchestral music, isolating unnecessary duplications where one instrumental part simply doubles another. Some of the pieces in this book may give an idea of how this can be done economically.

The
Sequences

Sequence 1
Prelude

A prelude is a curtain-raiser – sometimes to an opera or a suite of short pieces. Kreisler's intriguing Prœludium and Allegro, from which this sequence is taken, is a synthesis of musical styles from several different periods, making it a perfect all-purpose introduction to a collection of sequenced classics. Although it was written for a simple combination of violin and piano, the grand style suggests it would benefit from the full synth treatment.

Fritz Kreisler

Kreisler was one of the most notable violinists of the 20th century, achieving an international reputation through his world tours. He had an undisguised hatred of modern music, which hardly ever appeared in his programmes. He did, however, play a number of attractive little pieces by various 18th-century composers to which, curiously, nobody else seemed to have access.

In 1935 Kreisler admitted to an impressively sustained hoax. This *Prœludium and Allegro* "by Pugnani" (a genuine 18th-century violinist-composer) was actually Kreisler's own composition, along with a host of other fakes that he had been playing regularly in public.

Critics, as is their wont, were scandalized. However, perhaps the joke was on them for failing to spot that Kreisler's "olden style" had little in common with genuine 18th-century music. The rhythms are too static, the chords just a little too rich, as a quick comparison with some of the pieces later in this book will show. Genuine or not, this piece has become a favourite *encore* item.

Recording

The simple patterns on all three tracks should not present many rhythmic problems, and they may benefit from a tight quantization to quarter-notes. The wide leaps in Track 1 are much easier to perform on the violin than on the keyboard – you could try using both hands to play this part. Step-writing is also an option, particularly since the note lengths seldom vary.

The *8va* sign covers music that should sound an octave higher than written. Any such notes will need to be **transposed** up 12 semitones on the sequencer if your keyboard does not extend far enough.

Kreisler marked the speed as *Allegro* (fast), but violinists almost always exercise their artistic license in this work, and squeeze as much grandeur as possible from the music by taking it at about 72 bpm (beats per minute).

Præludium

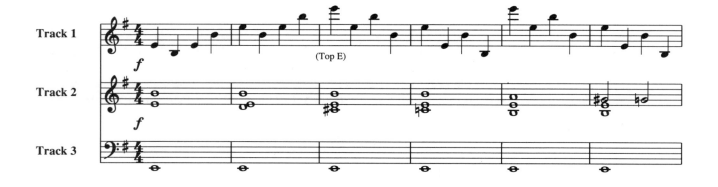

TIP The chords on Track 2 have been slightly simplified from the original, but may still be difficult to play accurately in real time. Most sequencers have an **overdub** facility which allows new notes to be recorded on a track without erasing existing material. The chords could therefore be built up in layers, recording all the top notes first, then the middle notes and so on.

BASS PART

The leaps in Track 1 and the chord changes in Track 2 are likely to result in notes shorter than are indicated by the score. In this piece, although by no means in all music, fully sustained note-lengths (*legato*) will sound good. Use a **note-length quantize** to eliminate any gaps but avoid overlapping, as synths cannot produce an unlimited number of simultaneous notes. Kreisler notated the original bass part in octaves: sequencer users can simply make a copy of Track 3, transpose it down 12 semitones and set it to the same MIDI channel as the original track. Although these notes are very low, synths can usually play sounds well beyond the range of their keyboards.

VOICING

The piece could be voiced to reflect the original scoring of violin on Track 1 and piano on Tracks 2 and 3. However, string sounds are not always produced convincingly by synths and, in any case, the music will respond well to a much more elaborate voicing. Some options include a sustained, resonant bass, shimmering chords and a celestial-sounding voice for the melody line – or perhaps a mix of punchy analogue synth sounds. Take the opportunity to explore some of those voices that you thought you would never use!

If your system has sufficient multi-timbral capacity, you could further enrich the texture by making copies of all three tracks and assigning these to an extra set of voices, perhaps transposing some of the lines to different octaves. Further ideas for a totally different approach to voicing are given *below*.

Creative voicing

In each of the sequences in this book we have given the composer's original instrumentation and have suggested ways in which the synth user can recreate these sounds. However, this is not the only – nor necessarily the most effective – way to sequence the classics. Many of the great synthesists, from Walter Carlos and Tomita onwards, have produced totally new interpretations of classical music that exploit the capabilities of electronic sound rather than imitating live instruments.

Creating a truly individual arrangement can be one of the most exciting parts of sequencing. One possibility for getting started is to forget any preconceived notion of how the music *ought* to sound and then find voices that suit the character of the main melody. Don't feel obliged to keep to one single voice throughout, even if the original does.

Concentrate on the bass part next. A **bass guitar** voice will immediately give a much punchier quality than the traditional bowed basses of the classical orchestra, although it may make more impact in slow music if you liven up the part to give a "classic rock" treatment. This might include repeating notes or outlining chord shapes in the bass, and syncopating the rhythm by moving some of the main notes half a beat early. Try adding a drum pattern at this point: it may spark off a whole lot of new ideas.

Possible choices for sustained backing parts might include colours that the original composer never even dreamt of – an angelic **choir**, **warm pad** or stratospheric swirl of some sort. Faster moving parts, though, will need to be taken by more immediate sounds such as **vibes**, **marimba** or **strat** guitar.

Sequence 2
Sumer Is Icumen In

Only in the last 150 years has there been much interest in any music of the past. Before that, musical taste was dominated by contemporary fashions and even masters like Bach and Vivaldi were quickly forgotten after their deaths. The wealth of music from the middle ages remained virtually unheard until much more recently, when performances on reconstructed medieval instruments began to reveal sounds and textures of completely unexpected vitality and expressiveness. The three pieces in this chapter date from the 13th and 14th centuries, and are among the earliest surviving examples of non-religious European music.

This round was written down by a monk of Reading Abbey in about 1250, soon after the signing of Magna Carta. It is a unique survival from the period in its complexity and modern-sounding harmony and the lyrics are among the very earliest examples of English verse.

Sumer Is Icumen In — Anonymous (13th Century)

TIP The $\frac{6}{8}$ time-signature indicates six eighth-notes per bar, divided into two groups of three as shown *left*. If your metronome insists on beating every one of these six pulses, you may find it easier to use the two beats in a bar supplied by $\frac{2}{4}$ time, dividing them into threes by ear.

After recording this melody, make three copies onto separate tracks and stagger these at two-bar intervals as shown on the layout diagram *opposite*.

Another tiny round in two parts repeats throughout the piece, forming an ingenious *ostinato* accompaniment. This was engagingly called the *Pes* (or "feet") in the original manuscript and should be recorded onto Track 5:

Repeat this pattern seven more times. Then copy all 32 bars into Track 6, but starting two bars later to form the subsidiary round:

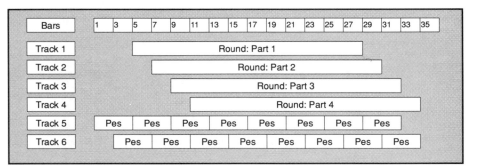

VOICING

You could try to reproduce the homogenous effect of six singers or each track might be voiced to an appropriately medieval sound. Authentic 13th-century timbres include:

Shawm	a kind of rough oboe sound
Flageolet	a shrill flute or whistle sound
Recorder	a more hollow flute or panpipes sound
Bells	tuned handbells were hugely popular
Harp or **Guitar**	less resonant than their modern equivalents
Rebec or **Vielle**	light, bowed string sounds suitable for the *Pes*

Triangle

Tambourine

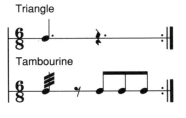

Various percussion instruments were also used, although never notated in the music. These include triangle, castanets, tambourine and tabor (a small drum). A simple suggestion to repeat throughout this sequence is shown *left*. The note with three beams through its stem indicates eight repeated thirty-second notes: with luck, this should give you a tambourine shake!

TEMPO

Early music never included speed directions: try a tempo of about 112 bpm so that the earthy Middle English lyrics of the round can be sung comfortably:

Sumer is icumen in
Lhude sing cuccu!
Groweth sed and bloweth med
And springth the wde nu.
      Sing cuccu!
	Summer is a-coming in
	Loudly sing cuckoo!
	Seeds are growing, meadows flow' ring
	Woods spring up anew.
	      Sing cuckoo!

Awe bleteth after lomb, Lhouth after calve cu. Bulluc sterteth, Bucke verteth: Murie sing cuccu!	*Ewes are bleating after lambs,* *Cows after calves do moo.* *Bulls are starting, Deer are farting:* *Merry sing, cuckoo!*
Cuccu, cuccu, Wel singes thu cuccu. Ne swik thu naver nu!	*Cuckoo, cuckoo,* *Well do you sing, cuckoo.* *Don't stop whatever you do!*

Medieval Dances

13th century music tends to use only a very small number of predetermined rhythm patterns, for no means had yet been discovered of showing individual note-lengths. By the 14th century, the basis of our modern system of rhythmic notation had been established, allowing composers much wider scope for expression. This change in style is evident in the slow Italian dance, *overleaf:*

The Lament of Tristan

A

B

A¹

This wistful, folk-like melody from the time of Chaucer's Canterbury Tales perhaps conveys the misery of the middle ages, with all its plagues and oppression, more than any of the noble knights and fairy-tale castles that fill the story books.

The music is **monophonic** (single line) but may well have been accompanied by a soft **drone** (continuous note). Try a low A, or perhaps A and D together. The fingering suggestions include two different methods for shifting the hand into new positions in the smoothest way possible (*see left*).

The composer is again unknown, but the piece was evidently written in Italy for the vielle, an early form of viola. There are three repeated sections: most of the third could be copied from section A. Notice that each section has an alternative ending for its repeat, known as a **second-time** bar. A slow tempo and minimal quantization will help preserve the expressive line.

RIGHT HAND

Developments

Early music is not easy to obtain, except in rare and expensive scholarly editions. To conclude this chapter, we have therefore included the music of another medieval dance, which happens to be preserved in the same British Museum manuscript as *Sumer Is Icumen In*.

The **Ductia** was one of the most popular medieval dance forms, consisting of four lively repeating sections. Some copyable patterns are shown in the score, although you may find others that can be adapted. *Sumer Is Icumen In* will provide ideas for voicing and percussion parts. A drone on a low G could be added if the background hum of your equipment is not already loud enough!

Copy of bars 1-4 in Track 2

Copy of bars 1-8 in Track 2, transposed up 7 semitones

Copy of bars 9-16 in Track 2, transposed up 7 semitones

EARLY NOTATION

Although music has undoubtedly been made since the dawn of civilization, the lack of an accurate system of notation means there is no possibility of knowing how this very early music would have sounded.

The evolution of music notation in Europe began around 850AD in the monasteries and universities, where the church not only had a monopoly on learning, but also a need to record its music for dissemination and for posterity. This may explain why so much church music has been preserved from the middle ages while the smaller number of non-religious pieces have survived almost by accident.

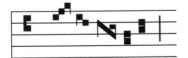

The original notation of the start of this piece looked like the example, *left*. The stylized C at the start, indicating Middle C, is a clef while the square shape of the notes themselves simply results from using a quill pen.

A system of lines and spaces to represent pitch had come into use before 1066, although early staves had a variable number of lines to suit the range of the music. Rhythm patterns, however, were shown only by the grouping of notes rather than by individual note-shapes. Time signatures, regular bar-lines and any indications of how to perform the music did not appear until much later.

Sequence 3
Virginals, Voices and Venetian Brass

The discovery of maritime routes both to the Far East and the Americas in the 15th Century resulted in an explosion of European trade. Cities like Venice prospered as money was poured into the building and decoration of churches and palaces. A newly-rich merchant class, eager to enjoy both its wealth and leisure time, began to rival church and court as patrons of the arts. Alongside music written for the grand ceremonies of the church, new pieces began to appear designed specifically for more intimate domestic performance. The invention of music printing around 1500 enabled composers to reach a far wider market. This remarkable flowering in every area of the arts became known as the Renaissance – a rebirth of the cultural ideals of the ancient world.

Elizabethan Virginal Music

The years around 1600 were one of the great periods in English music. The piece *opposite* is by Giles Farnaby, a contemporary of Shakespeare. It was written for the virginals, an early form of harpsichord and one of the favourite instruments of the cultured amateur keen to make music at home.

Much English virginal music has survived thanks to the efforts of one such enthusiast, Francis Tregian, who copied out nearly 300 pieces to pass the time while in jail for his Roman Catholic beliefs. This collection is now known as the *Fitzwilliam Virginal Book*.

Bars 5-8 and 17-24 are decorated repeats of the preceding music. In the second of these, the lower parts actually remain the same and can therefore be copied.

ORNAMENTS

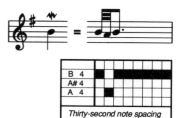

Thirty-second note spacing

Most virginal pieces are liberally scattered with signs for ornaments, although it is not always clear how these were played. We have indicated a few possibilities in the score, using an equivalent modern symbol. These should be interpreted as shown *left*.

Ornaments can be difficult to play and they need a much finer quantize resolution than the longer notes which form the bulk of the track. They do, however, add much to the character of this type of music.

TIP Try recording Track 1 unornamented. Then step-write the first ornament onto a different track. Copy this into the relevant bars, moving patterns to new pitches where required. Those in bars 2 and 10 should use C and B (not A#) in order to stay in the key of G. Set this new track to the same MIDI channel as Track 1 so that the ornaments totally integrate with the original material.

Most of the pieces in the *Fitzwilliam Virginal Book* are characterized by an additional final chord in a bar of its own. This is often elaborately spread (arpeggiated) in performance. Here, each note-start could be staggered by as much as an eighth-note – or you might even substitute a short improvisation on the notes of a G major chord.

VOICING

A harpsichord or perhaps guitar voice would sound good on all tracks – more sustained voices may need shortened note-lengths to sound effective. Many harpsichord presets are programmed to sound an octave lower than the light tone produced by the virginals. If the sequence sounds muddy on playback you can always transpose it up an octave.

Tracks 2 and 3 repeat bars 9-16

TEMPO

Renaissance music still did not include any tempo markings, although the contemporary composer Tomkins wrote that the semibreve (whole-note) should equal two beats of a man's heart. Assuming he was not exposed to undue excitement at the time, this would suggest a speed of about 152 bpm.

MUSIC IN STEREO

Andrea Gabrieli was organist at the Basilica of St Mark's in Venice from 1566 until his death in 1586. He was particularly famous for his ceremonial pieces, including church and instrumental music in up to twelve parts. The musicians were often divided into two groups which were placed in opposite galleries in St Mark's to achieve a stereophonic effect.

TIP Set each track to a different MIDI channel, even if you use the same brass voice on each. This will prevent certain long notes from being clipped by note-off signals when an adjacent part contains a shorter version of the same note (*eg* the Middle C shared by Horn and Trombone in bar 4).

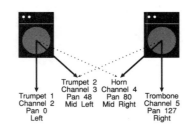

This sequence will benefit from panning Tracks 1 and 2 to the left and Tracks 3 and 4 to the right. Some sequencers offer **Pan** as one of the track settings or as part of a graphic MIDI mixing desk. Alternatively, you may be able to write a pan setting of between 0 and 127 as a MIDI message (Controller 10) at the very beginning of each track.

If your synth is not designed to respond to these MIDI pan messages you could try panning each part of your multi-timbral patch to create an all-purpose stereo spectrum which can be saved for future sequences. Voices can then be placed in position by assigning appropriate MIDI channels on the sequencer.

This Ricercare, just the first part of which is printed below, was written by Gabrieli for the resonating spaces of St Mark's. If you have an effects unit, use a **large hall** setting with a decay time of as much as 10 seconds. The long reverb time should not mean, however, that the piece is played slowly: choose a speed fast enough to sound like two, rather than four beats in a bar.

Developments

Much of the music of the renaissance was written primarily to be sung rather than played. A huge number of madrigals, motets and masses have survived, although not all such vocal music sequences successfully. The following *Canon à ronde* may have been intended for either voices or instruments, although here it is set to the word "Sanctus" from the mass. It was written by the curiously named Clemens non Papa, who died in 1570, and captures much of the linear beauty of the polyphonic style.

Record the single melody and copy it onto four other tracks, staggering the starts at two-bar intervals to form the round. At least one of the tracks could be transposed down an octave for variety. Voicing, and therefore speed, will depend largely on the choir-type voices on your synth.

As in the last sequence, cathedral-length reverb will enhance this music. Remember that in live performance you normally hear more direct than reflected sound. Balancing dry sound to effects in a ratio of about 6:4 should prevent the dreaded swimming bath effect.

Synth workstations often include an effects section which allows reverb to be added to individual voices, or to the output of your whole multi-timbral patch. *See* page 84 for further details.

Sanctus
Clemens non Papa

Sanc - - - - tus, Sanc - - - - tus, Sanc -

- - - - tus, Sanc - - - - - tus, Sanc - - tus.

FURTHER SEQUENCING

The *Fitzwilliam Virginal Book* is published in two (rather large) volumes. The following pieces from Book II are worth trying:

Giles Farnaby	*A Toye* [Nº 270]
Martin Peerson	*The Fall of the Leafe* [Nº 272]
William Byrd	*Coranto* [Nº 218]

Much of Gabrieli's instrumental music for St Mark's has been published; two other fine collections, although not always easy to find, are:

Tylman Susato	*Danserye*
Michael Praetorius	*Terpsichore*

Renaissance madrigals are readily available in paperback collections. The lighter ones, known as Balletts (with their inevitable fa-la-la refrains) should sequence particularly well: look out for those by the English composers, Morley and Weelkes.

Sequence 4
Music for the Stage

While the English madrigal remained a source of domestic leisure, the Italians took matters much more seriously. Paid singers were employed and dancing, instrumental music, costumes and elaborate staging were added to produce dramatic extravaganzas for aristocratic pleasure. Spurred on by the renaissance ambition to recreate the combination of dance, music and poetry in ancient Greek drama, these elements were integrated by 1600 under an umbrella word of the greatest significance – Opera.

Opera did not remain the preserve of the wealthy aristocracy for long. The first public opera house opened in 1637 and the craze for opera soon spread to other parts of Europe. The implications were enormous: not only did opera generate new ways of composing, but its very existence created a demand for professional singers and permanent instrumental ensembles – the first orchestras – that was to move music into a new and more commercial domain.

Monteverdi

Claudio Monteverdi is credited with producing the first real opera, *Orfeo,* in 1607. The introductory Toccata, *overleaf,* is a fanfare based on a single chord. It seems to herald a new, grandly ornate style known as the Baroque which was to dominate European culture for the next 150 years.

Orfeo is one of the first pieces to use a recognizable orchestra, including:

2 recorders
2 cornetts (high wooden instruments with trumpet-like mouth-pieces)
5 trumpets
5 trombones
14 bowed string instruments of various sizes

Multiple instruments often play the same parts in orchestral music to produce a rich texture and adequate volume. However, a similar effect can be achieved on the synth without needing 30 or more separate tracks: use voices such as strings or brass that will each reproduce the sound of a full orchestral section.

Record all four parts on separate tracks and copy them twice to give the three repetitions that Monteverdi asks for. The first play-through could be assigned to brass and the second to woodwind. To get the effect of a full orchestra for the final repeat you will need to make parallel copies of all four tracks, assigning one set to strings, another to brass and a third to woodwind voices.

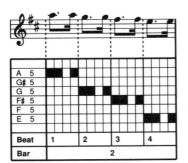

In addition, the notes in Track 4 would have been improvised upon by an army of other instruments, including harpsichords, lutes, bass viols (like cellos), archcitterns (low plucked strings), harp and organ. Aim for a minimum of one plucked and one bowed sound on this part – a tremolo strumming effect would also be appropriate if your synth has a **mandolin** or **koto** voice. At least two extra copies of Track 4 will be needed to carry this accompaniment.

TIP Much of the music will benefit from shorter note-lengths than those written *(staccato)*. This is particularly important in the dotted eighth-note patterns in bar 2 *(see left)*. Try a playback speed of around 112 bpm. Effects will depend largely on the voices used, but note that this piece was not written for church performance and would have been heard in relatively dry acoustics.

Toccata *from* Orfeo

Henry Purcell

The rigours of Cromwell's puritanism delayed the arrival of opera in England. However, after the restoration of the monarchy in 1660 an audience starved of entertainment crowded to the newly reopened theatres. Plays with specially composed musical interludes, dances and songs became popular as an English substitute for the entirely musical format of Italian opera.

Henry Purcell was organist at Westminster Abbey and in 1695, shortly before his death, he was commissioned to write the incidental music for *Abdelazer, or The Moor's Revenge* by Mrs. Aphra Behn, former spy in Antwerp for Charles II and highly successful playwright.

A rondeau (**rondo**) is a piece in which a main section alternates with other material in an A-B-A-C-A pattern. The Rondeau *below* would have been played by a small string ensemble reinforced by harpsichord. However, it will bear a much grander arrangement, as Benjamin Britten discovered in 1946 with his variations on the piece in *The Young Person's Guide to the Orchestra*.

Note that the piece is in $\frac{3}{4}$ time and that, in the loud sections, Track 4 would be augmented by double basses sounding an octave lower. In Purcell's time the contrast in the softer sections would have been emphasized by using fewer players – or you could try different voices such as flute, oboe and bassoon.

Rondeau *from* Abdelazer — Purcell

B

After this, section A (bars 1-8) should be repeated to form bars 17-24 of the rondo before recording section C *below*.

TIP Some string voices respond so slowly that it can be hard to synchronize with the metronome beat when recording. For once, it may be easier to use a clearer voice and then assign the tracks to strings on playback.

If you use the same voice for the top two tracks, set them to different MIDI channels to prevent the problem of note-clipping mentioned in Sequence 3.

C

The rondo finishes with a final repeat of section A. The *tr* above indicates a **trill** – a rapid alternation between A and G in this instance. Six thirty-second notes, followed by the printed F and G, should give the right effect.

Choosing the right tempo is one of the performer's most important decisions. Here, 76 bpm will give the music a noble grandeur, while 112 bpm will reveal a surprisingly dance-like character.

Developments

FIGURED BASS

Baroque ensembles almost always included a harpsichord or organ, although this keyboard part was seldom notated in full. The player was expected to improvise an accompaniment using the bass line as a guide. Numbers were added to this to remind the player of the basic harmony. This system, known as **figured bass**, had a similar shorthand function to a modern lead sheet with chord symbols.

CONTINUO

The partnership of improvised keyboard part and bass instrument(s) was called the *continuo,* from its continual presence in almost all music of the period – even in passages where the rest of the orchestra were silent.

In *Music in Sequence* we described how an acceptable continuo part can be made by merging some of the existing parts onto a special harpsichord track. This quick and easy technique could be used here, perhaps **merging** just the lower three parts – note that the resulting hybrid track may have to be reduced in volume to keep the harpsichord in the background. However, you may wish to experiment with a truly improvised continuo, in which case the example *below* shows one of many ways in which a keyboard player might elaborate the first two bars of the piece:

Sequence 5
Royal Commissions

No one better illustrates the growing commercial status of the baroque musician than Handel. Born and trained in Germany, he travelled to Italy at the age of 21 to be at the source of new musical developments. While enjoying considerable success at the opera in Venice he was head-hunted to become director of music at the court of the Elector of Hanover. His Italian reputation also resulted in invitations to England where, during one visit in 1714, he learned that his employer had succeeded to the English throne as George I. Never slow to cash in on royal connections, Handel became a British citizen and the natural choice as a composer of music for state occasions. He remained based in London for the rest of his life, where he made (and lost) several fortunes investing in the production of his own operas and oratorios.

Music for the Royal Fireworks

The *Music for the Royal Fireworks* was commissioned for a grand spectacle in 1749 to celebrate the short-lived Peace of Aix-la-Chappelle: one of those treaties more of political importance than of any lasting effect.

A measure of Handel's popularity at this time is given by the fact that 12,000 people converged on Vauxhall Gardens for a public rehearsal of the piece, causing a 3-hour jam of horse-drawn carriages on London Bridge. The actual performance in Green Park was rather more successful than the accompanying fireworks, which exploded prematurely and set light to the staging.

The bourrée *opposite* is just one of a set of dances in the score. Such **suites** were popular as harpsichord pieces, although some were written for orchestra. Here, the outdoor performance called for a large wind band – Handel's intention also to include strings was firmly quashed by George II who asked for military instruments and "hoped there would be no fidles" in the orchestra. The original scoring of the bourrée was for two oboe parts with bassoon bass.

RECORDING

The dance suite provided a framework of short, highly contrasted movements, each with its own rhythmic style and almost always in two repeated sections. The bourrée was particularly lively; the ¢ time signature indicates a feel of two strong beats per bar – $\frac{2}{2}$ rather than $\frac{4}{4}$ if your sequencer allows this setting. Try a speed of 116 bpm (232 bpm in $\frac{4}{4}$ time).

TIP Tight quantization will highlight the insistent baroque rhythms and Handel's characteristic "walking bass" of regular quarter-notes in Track 3. Sequencer users can give much eighteenth century music an even more lively Classic Rock treatment by the addition of electric bass and a drum track.

Track 1: Bar 7

Notice that both sections start at the end of bars. Because of these upbeats, take care to avoid unwanted gaps or overlaps if you copy the repeats rather than playing them live. A slight *rit.* (slowing down) will help round off the final two bars of the piece: this is usually done on a tempo mastertrack.

TIP Your performance will really come to life if there is a sharp contrast between the **staccato** (detached) and **legato** (smooth) playing of small groups of notes. The precise distribution of these effects should remain a matter for personal experiment, although the long notes will sound best if given their full value. You might try making all quarter-notes *staccato* except when they form parts of descending scales, as in bar 5 of Track 3 or as shown *left*.

Bourrée *from* **The Fireworks Music**

The Arrival of the Queen of Sheba

Midway through Handel's career the popularity of opera in Italian began to wane with London audiences. Faced with financial ruin, Handel created a new and more accessible musical form: English **oratorio**. These were large scale concert pieces for chorus, solo singers and orchestra which narrated familiar biblical stories in a language that the public could understand.

Handel's oratorios, and in particular *Messiah,* rapidly became so popular that he stopped writing opera altogether and set himself to satisfy this new public demand. *Solomon* was written in 1748 and contains an orchestral movement entitled Sinfonia, now better known as the *Arrival of the Queen of Sheba*.

RECORDING

Handel gives a tempo marking of ***Allegro*** (fast) – about 104 bpm. Put some bounce in the rhythm by imagining a stronger pulse on beats one and three than on the others when recording.

Although the music is laid out on five staves, you will need seven or possibly eight tracks, voiced as follows:

Track 1	**Oboe 1**	(stave 1)
Track 2	**Oboe 2**	(stave 2)
Track 3	**Violins**	(stave 3)
Track 4	**Violas**	(stave 4)
Track 5	**Cellos**	(stave 5)
Track 6	**Double Bass**	(Track 5 transposed down 12 semitones)
Track 7	**Bassoon**	(a duplicate of Track 5)
Track 8	**Harpsichord**	(a merge of Tracks 4 and 5)

Track 7 is optional, but it reflects the standard baroque practice of having a bassoon play off the bass part whenever oboes were present in the orchestra. A harpsichord (or organ) would have partnered the cellos – a realistic effect can be achieved by merging some of the string parts onto a new track, re-voiced appropriately. A live continuo player would not include all the sixteenth-notes in the violin part, although only perfectionists will wish to experiment much with this!

The main melody here is played by the violins, as in so much orchestral music. Handel does not suggest any **dynamics** (volume levels) but the music for full orchestra should be a robust ***forte*** (loud). The dynamics of other sections can be terraced to enhance the changes in texture. In particular, the short string episodes at bars 20 and 26 could be ***piano*** (soft) to contrast with the opening.

TIP It is often easier to adjust volume levels for each section *after* recording, by using a velocity edit function. This method will obviously be essential if your keyboard is not touch sensitive. You will also find that the constant eighth-notes in the two lowest tracks will sound good *staccato*.

STRUCTURE

The Sinfonia is in **ritornello** form – a development of the rondo form seen in the last chapter – in which only selected parts of the first section are repeated, some in different keys from the original. Although frustrating for copying enthusiasts, the resulting variety makes the music much more interesting.

The entire piece is too long to print here but you can use a copy of bars 7-16 to make an effective ending, as Handel himself does to conclude the full 90 bars of the original. The term ***Dal Segno al fine*** (sometimes abbreviated to ***D.S.***) at the end of the extract is an instruction to repeat the music from the special sign (in bar 7) to the word ***fine*** (finish).

Sinfonia *from* Solomon

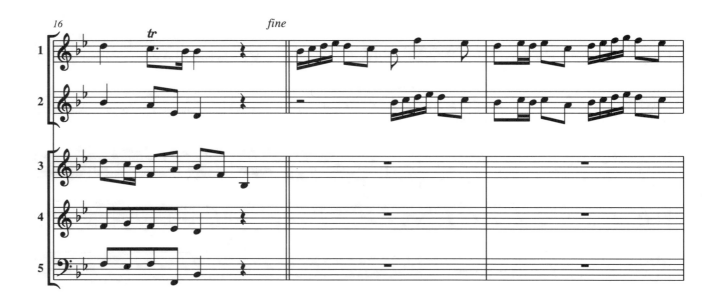

Dal Segno al fine

Developments

FURTHER SEQUENCING

Other music written in England at this time includes:

Handel   *Fireworks Music* (La Réjouissance and Menuet II)
Handel   *Water Music* (Air, Bourrée and Hornpipe)
Handel   Organ Concertos (particularly Nº 3 in F)
Jeremiah Clarke   Trumpet Voluntary

More music by Handel and other baroque composers appears later in the book.

Sequence 6
Two Baroque Cameos

Alongside public music on a grand scale, the quiet growth of amateur music making created a demand for smaller, intimate pieces which no baroque composer could afford to ignore. Bach, Handel, Vivaldi and their contemporaries produced countless pieces for small groups of players and for solo harpsichord. Although many of these are simply called Sonata or Suite, French composers such as Couperin and Rameau started to explore the descriptive powers of music, using evocative titles like Le Rossignol en amour (The Nightingale in love) and L'Egyptienne (The Egyptian Girl).

The Gigue *below* is taken from a set of twelve sonatas by Handel for "recorder, flute, oboe or violin with continuo" – a wide range of instruments clearly intended to achieve maximum sales with minimum effort. Handel squeezed further mileage from the music when he later arranged it for organ and strings – he was never afraid to rework his own (or other composers') best material.

The music was first published about 1730, printed on just two staves, as it is here. The harpsichord player would, as usual, be expected to make up an additional part from the bass line. You will probably find that the bass will work perfectly well on its own, perhaps voiced for bassoon.

The first eighth-note of each group of six will sound good played full length, but most notes need to be *staccato*. Try a speed of 124 bpm: if the $\frac{12}{8}$ time gives an unwieldy number of beats on your metronome, use $\frac{4}{4}$ and subdivide into threes by ear. Remember to quantize to 8T (or 12) if you do this.

Gigue *from* **Sonata in F**   **Handel**

Daquin, a contemporary of Handel, was considered to be the outstanding French keyboard player of the time. The title of this famous harpsichord piece leaves little room for doubt that the music is based on the call of a cuckoo.

Le Coucou is in rondo form: record and copy out the sections as shown *below*. In the final repeat of A² the bass E (bar 115) should be lengthened to match the chord above it. The remaining seven bass notes will need to be erased.

Bars	1 - 11	12 - 23	24 - 42	43 - 53	54 - 65	66 - 92	93 - 103	104 - 115
Section	A¹	A²	B	A¹	A²	C	A¹	A²

The ornaments *(see left)* are probably best ignored until after the basic music has been recorded and quantized. Using the technique explained on page 24, the first ornament can be recorded or step-written onto a fresh track. This can then be copied and transposed into the relevant bars. When the ornament is used on F#, as in bars 10 and 22, its upper note will be G rather than G#.

F#5						
F 5						
E 5						

Thirty-second note spacing

Allegro [138 bpm]

FURTHER SEQUENCING

Other harpsichord music that should sequence well includes movements from Bach's English and French Suites and any of his Two-Part Inventions.

Also explore the many trio sonatas by Vivaldi and Telemann as well as some of the other movements in Handel's set of twelve solo sonatas, opus 1.

Fact Sheet
Voicing the Classics

Music that was originally written for acoustic instruments poses special challenges for the synth user. Even at the recording stage, passages that would come easily to, say, a violinist using a bow can be far more awkward to accomplish smoothly on the keyboard. A flute or oboe part may sound unconvincing because you have forgotten to make space between the phrases where the original player would need to breathe. Really heavy quantizing, particularly of note-lengths and velocities, can rob the music of all its subtlety and interest.

Once you have a track input exactly as you want it, you may still find that your synth's violin, flute or oboe voices, if it has them at all, do not sound remotely like the real thing. This chapter is about voicing – making the best use of your instrument, as classical composers had to with the resources at their disposal, so that the music itself comes across with freshness and vitality.

Composers of classical music use a palette of clearly distinguishable sounds which will nonetheless blend together. There will almost certainly be versions of these acoustic timbres on the voice list of the average synth. However, these voices are likely to vary widely in their suitability for different types of music. If your aim is to make the sequences sound as realistic as possible, here are some suggestions for getting the best out of your synth.

WOODWIND

Woodwind instruments are often given prominent solo parts, so it is worth getting to know all of the options on your synth's voice list before making final decisions. Remember also that the way you record the part will be influenced by the response of the voice you choose.

Many synths include a **pan flute** or **bottle flute** which sounds breathier than the orchestral version but may work well, especially in fast or staccato music. **Double reed** is a composite name for both oboe and bassoon sounds, although a soft **tenor sax** may be more realistic on high bassoon solos. Substitutes for the clarinet are harder to find, especially as the acoustic instrument has three quite distinct timbres across its range, but a soft **alto sax** may help.

BRASS

Synths usually offer a wide range of brass sounds, but these will not all have been designed for classical sequencing. Anything labelled **syn brass** or **digihorn** is likely to sound heavily processed but may be useful as a substitute for *muted* trumpets or horns. A choice of soft and bright brass voices is helpful since the tone of a live instrument changes markedly as its volume increases: playing a mellow voice loudly on the synth will not give the same intensity as using a naturally loud brass voice at mid-level. Note that trumpets before about 1750 had a thinner but brighter tone than later instruments.

The french horn is much more mellow than the trumpet. The tone is very distinctive in solo parts, where a specific **french horn** voice would be helpful, but horns are often used simply to fill in the harmonies; here a softly blending, all-purpose **brass** or **tubaflugel** voice may sound better.

The trombone can be bright, mellow, dark or gruff – one single voice may not be enough for all purposes. A low trumpet will work for some passages, but at other times a **'bone** voice with a softer, richer character will be needed.

TIP Always be aware whether your chosen brass voice is programmed to sound like a solo instrument or several instruments playing together. Brass ensemble voices are fine for inner parts that merely support the harmonies, but a solo line clearly demands a solo-sounding voice.

STRINGS

String instruments play a very prominent rôle in classical music. Many string voices have too gritty an attack for gentle passages while others speak too slowly for fast music – a real headache for the synth user. This situation may be improved by voice editing *(see overleaf)* but most sequencers offer a simple solution to the problem of slow-speaking voices with a **delay** function.

This allows a value to be set by which a track is delayed relative to the rest of the sequence. A negative number, to *advance* a slow speaking track, will be needed here to synchronize the strings with more immediate voices. Delay does not alter note positions, as in quantizing, but merely outputs the track early or late, allowing settings to be changed instantly for different voices.

Pizzicato (plucked) string parts will often work very well on **guitar**, **harp** or **fretless bass** voices if you do not have a separate **pizz** string program.

Doubles basses usually play an octave below the cellos if no separate part is provided in the score – their low pitch is important to bolster the low frequency end of the orchestral spectrum. You may find non-string bass voices that can achieve this more successfully. If you use small monitor speakers beware of over-compensating for their lack of bass response by pushing up the volume: the sequence will sound ludicrously bottom heavy on a different system.

PERCUSSION

Percussion instruments are generally used more sparingly in classical scores than they are in rock music. The most common are the timpani – low drums tuned to specific notes. Timps will not be found on a synth's drum kit as this will consist entirely of single-pitched sounds. However, many synths include a **timp** or other pitched drum sound as a separate voice. Further percussion techniques, such as cymbal crashes, will be dealt with in later sequences.

OTHER OPTIONS

Multi-purpose voices like **orchestra** or **strings 'n' wind** can sometimes be used to double existing tracks when a rich texture is needed. They will work less well on their own because they will play each orchestral part with the same sound, making it impossible to layer the different timbres.

SAMPLERS

The most realistic-sounding acoustic voices are produced by a process known as sampling. Rather than being synthesized electronically, individual notes across the range of a live instrument are recorded digitally. These are then regenerated by the synth. Some synths include sampled voices but the best resources for authentic classical sequencing are found on dedicated orchestral sample players containing a collection of professionally recorded samples.

ROM AND RAM CARDS

You may find that the basic voice list of your synth does not, in fact, offer sufficient voice options. Thousands of extra sounds are available for the most popular synths in the form of ROM (Read-Only Memory) cards or 3½ inch disks. It can sometimes be difficult for MIDI to access these external voices simultaneously with the synth's internal sounds. However, voices can usually be loaded from the card or disk into the synth to replace existing presets.

In order to do this it is necessary to switch off the memory protection on your synth's voices. In this state it is easy to erase the *entire* original set of voices accidentally, so **remember to make a copy of your synth presets** before you start any of these functions and to restore the memory protect when you have finished. ROM cards cannot record data, so your original voices will have to be dumped onto a RAM (Random Access Memory) card or floppy disk.

LIBRARIAN PROGRAMS

Few synths have built-in floppy disk drives, but voice data can be dumped via MIDI into a universal librarian program on the computer. These are included with most sequencer programs and enable you to assemble all your favourite sounds in one place. Librarians for specific synths are also available and have the advantage of allowing you to edit voices on screen. Some of these will operate in tandem with the main sequencer program on computers with sufficient memory, although a special linking program may be necessary.

It is surprising how few synth users bother to use their voice editing facilities. You may spend days perfecting the recording of a sequence – why forfeit the chance of getting exactly the right sounds to make a totally individual interpretation of the music?

Editing a voice, or even creating a new sound from scratch, is not so daunting a task as some synth manuals might lead you to think. By far the easiest way of working is to use a voice editing program on the computer. As with sequencing itself, the computer screen gives a much clearer visual indication of the process than can be obtained from the synth's tiny display.

In many cases, editing a voice to get exactly the response you want can be just a matter of "tweaking" a few parameters: identifying these is easier if you have a basic understanding of how sound synthesis works. The information *below* gives a brief introduction, but note that samplers produce their sounds in a rather different way, and editing these will often be restricted to the later stages of the processes described, from envelope generators onwards.

Sound, in its most basic form, is simply the frequent change in air pressure caused by a vibrating object. Represented graphically, the size (**amplitude**) of the resulting sound wave determines the loudness of the sound, while the speed of vibration (**frequency**) determines its pitch. The tone (**timbre**) of a sound depends upon the shape and material of the vibrating object, causing distinctive variations in the basic sound wave:

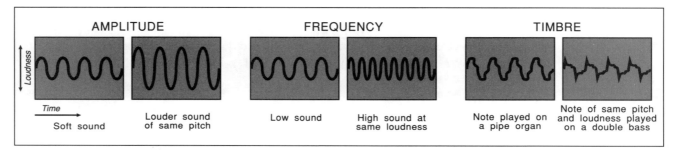

The human ear can hear musical notes at frequencies ranging from about 20 vibrations per second (20 Hertz) to about 16,000 Hz, although this upper limit decreases with age and exposure to loud disco music. Causing the air to vibrate at 256 Hz by, say, twanging a ruler of an appropriate length on a hard surface will produce the note Middle C. Doubling the speed of vibration will produce a pitch an octave higher while halving it gives a sound an octave lower.

The synth needs no such primitive means as a ruler to generate its vibrations. At its heart is an **oscillator** which generates rapidly changing voltage levels – the electronic version of a basic acoustic sound. This signal is then modified by a series of electronic circuits to produce the various pitches, timbres and volumes required. The result is amplified and finally turned into audible sound by the vibrating membrane of a loudspeaker:

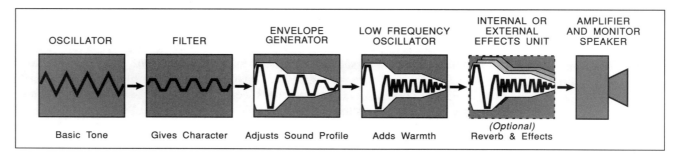

This is a highly simplified description of the synthesizing process. In reality, the synth is likely to have several oscillators interacting with each other, a variety of filters and envelope generators, various ways of controlling the response of the keyboard and – at least in the case of a workstation – a separate unit for adding reverb and other effects to the final sound.

OSCILLATORS

The alternating voltage levels generated by an oscillator can be set to change in a number of different ways. Each of the resulting waveforms will produce a distinctive raw tone colour. If the oscillator switches immediately between high and low voltages, a square wave is formed, giving a hollow, clarinet-like sound. A gradual shift between high and low levels produces a sine wave, with the pure but dull quality of an electronic whistle. Various combinations of jumping and ramping between high and low states will give other common waveforms, such as Sawtooth and Triangle waves, which provide the building blocks for brighter voices such as strings, trumpets and oboes:

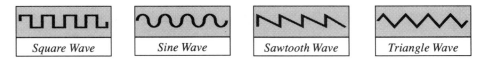

Square Wave   *Sine Wave*   *Sawtooth Wave*   *Triangle Wave*

The oscillator volume is set by a VDA (Variable Digital Amplifier) – altering this level will affect the fundamental intensity of the voice.

FILTERS

Filters are used to modify these waveforms by slicing away some of the waveshape to alter the tone. This adds a myriad of overtones to the basic sound which are not perceived as separate notes but instead give it a different character. The cut-off frequency of the filter will affect the overall brightness of the sound.

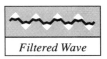

Filtered Wave

The process described here is known as subtractive synthesis – the filters subtract unwanted parts of the original waveform. Although new methods of sound generation have been developed with the advent of digital synths, such as modifying the waveform by *adding* data stored in memory, manufacturers usually retain the familiar editing terms of the analogue age.

ENVELOPES

So far, the process of synthesis may have produced an interesting tone colour, but its level is still absolutely constant throughout the duration of a note. In real life, a note may start suddenly, drop back to a plateau and eventually die away. This profile of a sound is known as the envelope and its parameters are set in the **envelope generator** (EG) section of the synth's edit system:

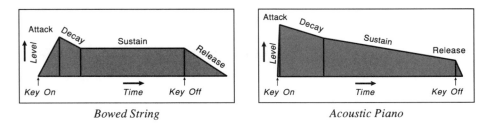

Bowed String   *Acoustic Piano*

Attack refers to the start of the note – how quickly (time) and loudly (level) it begins after a key is pressed. **Decay** is the speed and amount by which the sound drops back from this to its **Sustain** phase – the main part of the note. When the key is released, the way the sound ends is defined by the **Release** time and level. The piano has a fast, percussive attack as the hammer strikes the string, after which the sound steadily drops away. A bowed string takes longer to start speaking but its level remains constant for the rest of the note.

TIP Envelope editing can produce useful and effective results. For example, the string envelope *above* will speak too slowly for quick, bright music. Reducing the attack time and increasing its level will give notes a more immediate start, while reducing the release time will provide cleaner endings. Note that the edited voice may now prove too hard edged for soft, slow use.

As well as envelopes to adjust aspects of loudness, synths also provide **pitch envelopes** to take account of the tiny fluctuations in tuning that characterize the sound of many live instruments. For example, a timp will often sound slightly flat at the moment the stick hits the skin before returning to its main pitch level. Wild use of pitch EG can create a good rocket take-off impression!

LOW FREQUENCY OSCILLATORS

A **Low Frequency Oscillator** (LFO) is applied to the final sound to add **vibrato** (pitch modulation or fluctuation) and **tremolo** (volume fluctuation). Vibrato is used almost constantly by string players, while wind instruments often warm the sound with tremolo. Settings include the speed and depth of the modulation as well as its starting point in the note. Filters and envelopes are also often applied to the LFO to increase the subtlety of its effect.

Truly realistic synthesizing will take account of the fact that live players vary the speed and depth of their vibrato or tremolo continually. This calls for artistic use of the synth's modulation wheel and aftertouch as well as the voice's programmed modulation.

The application of LFO will also depend on the intended use of the voice – vibrato was merely an occasional ornament in string playing before 1750 while, by 1900, it was applied almost all the time. Similarly, brass players use much more vibrato in jazz or brass band playing than in orchestral work.

OTHER EDITING OPTIONS

A synth's editing facilities will include functions other than the ones given above. **Keyboard Tracking** sets the amount by which the synth automatically adjusts the envelope of a voice across its pitch range, allowing for the slower speaking characteristics of low sounds and the brighter attack of notes in the upper register. **Velocity Sensitivity** determines how the resulting voice will respond to key pressure.

Many voices are created by combining the sound from two or more oscillators or samples. There may be facilities to alter their relationship by **Cross-Fading** between them or by **Detuning** one of them to thicken the sound.

Output Level is used to set an overall volume for the voice which will match its characteristics. A very bright trumpet sound output at an unrealistically low level will give the impression of a loud instrument being played miles from the microphone. This will not sound the same as a soft trumpet. **Pan** settings will move the output between left and right on stereo synths.

Some synths combine Modulation and Pitchbend in a single Joystick control.

If your synth has **Aftertouch** or a **Modulation Wheel**, adjustments can be made to the speed, depth and startpoint of any additional vibrato or tremolo you want to apply to the voice with these controls. The width and direction of **Pitchbend** can also be set, usually up to 12 semitones above or below.

Finally, many synth users will have an **Effects** unit (sometimes part of the synth itself) for adding reverb and other kinds of electronic processing. Editing effects is a whole new topic which will be covered later in this book.

STORAGE

Your edits will be lost if they are not saved. However, you may not want to lose the original voice if it has worked well unaltered in previous sequences. The edited version should therefore be saved to an unwanted patch on your synth, or to a RAM card if you have one, or to floppy disk if using a librarian program. In addition, your synth manual may include a photocopyable sheet for keeping a written record of any changes you make while editing.

Sequence 7
High Baroque

The baroque style of music reached its maturity in the first half of the eighteenth century with the work of a host of major composers, most notably Bach, Handel and Vivaldi. After a century of development, from the time of Monteverdi, certain musical conventions had become firmly established. The tonal system had been developed to the point where related major and minor keys could be used to construct a complete movement from a single melodic idea. Continuity was reinforced by the constant repetition of distinctive short rhythm patterns providing a motor for the music. Finally, orchestration became more standardized, with a foundation of four string parts often overlaid by woodwind solos and with the occasional addition of trumpets and drums.

THE FOUR SEASONS

The four violin concertos by Vivaldi, collectively known as *The Four Seasons,* were written in Venice in 1725. Vivaldi was a master of the concerto form, in which the sound of one or more solo instruments contrasts with that of the full ensemble. The variety and quantity (nearly 500) of his concertos reflects the fact that he was employed for much of his life at the Pietà, an institution for training girl musicians, many of whom achieved considerable virtuosity.

Vivaldi was unusual amongst pre-19th century composers in attempting to describe scenes from everyday life in orchestral music. He prefaces each of the concertos in *The Four Seasons* with a sonnet setting out his extra-musical intentions. The central movement of Winter *(overleaf)* is described thus:

> *While streaming rain soaks the world outside,*
> *Quiet and peaceful days are spent by the fire.*

To portray the sound of raindrops, Vivaldi calls for plucked strings *(pizz.)* from the orchestral violins, while the other instruments play sustained lines with the bow *(arco)*. If you use a guitar or harp voice for the *pizzicato* parts, make several copies of these two tracks and fractionally delay or advance some of them to give the impression of the inevitably diffuse attack of an ensemble.

The original concerto was for violin. As noted earlier, this may not be the most rewarding timbre on the synth. Look for a solo voice which will respond readily to aftertouch modulation on the long notes and will react smoothly to the very *legato* playing needed. The orchestral accompaniment can be tightly quantized but leave the rhythm of the solo part free to be expressive. A *rit.* (gradual slowing down) could be applied to the last few notes of the piece.

TRILLS

Baroque trills traditionally start on the note of the scale above the one written, and at this speed will probably sound good as triplet thirty-seconds (32T). The final trill could finish with an eighth-note B at the very end of bar 17 to lead into the final note. Trills in slow music, and especially long trills, rarely keep to a constant speed. A live musician might perform the final trill like this:

D 5							
C# 5							
C 5							
B 4							
Beat	3	4	1	2	3	4	1
Bar		16			17		18

The original score was in Eb major, three semitones higher than the simpler key printed here. You might want to transpose the sequence back up to its original key, although rising pitch levels over the years mean that music of this period actually sounded at least two semitones lower than it would today.

Largo *from* "Winter" (The Four Seasons)

Vivaldi

Bach's church duties required him to supply a constant stream of choral and organ pieces for services. Consequently the opportunities for him to write purely orchestral music were much scarcer than they were for Vivaldi. In 1729, however, he enthusiastically took on the extra duties of running the *Collegium Musicum* in Leipzig, an informal society of professional and student musicians which performed weekly in a local coffee house. This suite of dances, which also includes the famous movement known as the "Air on a G String", was probably one of the first works that he wrote for the ensemble.

BAROQUE TRUMPETS

Baroque trumpets did not have valves and could therefore only play a limited number of notes. The length of the tube was generally designed to provide the main notes of D major. Players could, without the aid of a plumber, slot in extra sections of tube (called crooks) to play in other keys, but composers were mostly content to use the key of D major for music with trumpet parts.

Because trumpeters only had to think in one key at a time, their music was usually written in the key of C to avoid unnecessary sharps and flats. The key of the instrument automatically determines the pitches produced without the need for transposition by the player. Here we have printed the trumpet parts at pitch, although in other baroque scores you may have to transpose music for "Trumpets in D" up two semitones from C to D to avoid weird harmonies.

TIP The narrow bore of tubing used in baroque trumpets produced a brighter sound than that of more modern instruments. Try adjusting the filter cut-off point if the **trumpet** options on your synth seem too dull.

TIMPANI

Unlike most other drums, timpani produce clearly defined pitches. Kit drum sounds are generally too dry and pitchless to be adapted effectively. If you don't have a specific **timps** or perhaps **conga** voice that can play the notes required (D and A for this piece) you may wish to experiment with creating one from scratch as it will often be needed in orchestral sequencing.

RECORDING

In the original score, Bach included parts for two oboes which play the same music as the first violins. This track can be copied and voiced appropriately. The standard harpsichord continuo, although authentic, may not strike you as being essential for either of the pieces in this chapter.

As with other music that uses a cut C time-signature, the feel is of *two* beats per bar with notes on the intervening quarters played very lightly. Try a tempo of around 160 quarters (80 half-notes) per minute. Each section starts in the second half of a bar, so watch for gaps or overlaps when copying out repeats.

ORNAMENTS

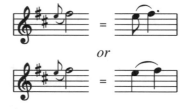

In bar 3 Bach includes an expressive grace note known as an *appoggiatura*. This always lasts for at least the length printed *(see left)*. Performers often added extra points of tension with ornaments of this kind, particularly on repeats. Composers also occasionally wrote them in – but using small print so as not to obscure the main harmony notes. The ornament could be adapted for use in similar places in the score, such as bars 7 and 21. The trills will probably sound quite fast enough using sixteenth-notes at this tempo.

TIP The shorter notes can be *staccato* to emphasize the dance rhythm. This is most simply achieved by careful recording although, if you are inputting at a very slow tempo, don't play too *staccato* or the notes will sound impossibly short at the proper speed. Alternatively, many sequencers offer a range of note-length quantizes, but some of these may also shorten the half-notes, which are here best left at full value. However, more complex functions, such as Logical Edit or Hyper-Edit, should allow you to exclude the long and trill notes when quantizing durations.

Gavotte I *from* Orchestral Suite Nº 3 in D — Bach

Developments

FURTHER SEQUENCING

The larger scale orchestral and choral works of the early eighteenth century include some of the most famous music of the baroque period. Among these, miniature scores of the following will provide good sequencing material:

Bach	Other movements from Orchestral Suite Nº 3 and dances from Orchestral Suite Nº 2 in B minor for flute and strings
Bach	6 *Brandenburg* Concertos – particularly Nº 2 in F
Bach	Violin Concertos in A minor and E
Bach	Concerto in D minor for two violins
Corelli	*Christmas* Concerto, Nº 8 from the 12 Concerti Grossi
Handel	Concerti Grossi, as well as the Suites and Concertos mentioned at the end of Sequence 5
Vivaldi	Concerto for two trumpets
Vivaldi	12 Concertos *L'Estro Harmonico* – try Nº 8 in A minor

The ever-popular *Adagio* "by Albinoni" is worth considering, although it is actually a 20th-century composition based on a fragment of original material. Baroque music for voices will also give scope for some creative sequencing. Try Vivaldi's *Gloria,* the opening of Handel's *Zadok the Priest,* movements from *Messiah* (perhaps "The Trumpet Shall Sound") and parts of the B minor Mass by Bach. The following two arias are among the most famous of hundreds of equally good movements from Bach's 200-plus cantatas:

"Sheep May Safely Graze" from Cantata Nº 208
"Jesu, Joy of Man's Desiring" from Cantata Nº 147

Sequence 8
Classical Music

Most people assume that the term classical music refers to all so-called "serious" music of the past. For musicians it specifically applies to the elegant and expressive style which developed out of the baroque around 1750 and dominated European musical culture for more than 70 years. The source of many of these developments was the group of composers working in and around Vienna – Haydn, Mozart, Beethoven and Schubert. Some features of the classical style may seem, on the surface, to be even more constrained and formal than those of the baroque – an increasing reliance on melody supported by purely functional bass parts, regular phrasing and simple key structures. However, in the hands of great composers, this superficial, aristocratic elegance often conceals an undercurrent seething with an expressive power whose drama seems to parallel the revolutions which were transforming society, particularly in France and in the New World.

Minuet in D K.355

> The K. numbers which identify Mozart's music were assigned by Köchel in 1862 to make up for the lack of opus numbers – the simple cataloguing system used by many other composers.

The Minuet, a slowish dance in $\frac{3}{4}$ time, was immensely fashionable in 18th-century Vienna. Mozart used the form throughout his career from his earliest keyboard compositions, and classical composers commonly included it as a movement in instrumental sonatas and orchestral symphonies.

The example *opposite,* with its chromatic writing and biting dissonances, is clearly not intended for actual dancing, but shows Mozart transforming an old form for his own expressive purposes. The original piano version was printed on two staves. Here we have expanded it onto three to highlight the individual lines of music, each of which could be assigned a different voice if you wish.

The symbol over the note in bar 4 and elsewhere indicates a **turn**. These are used to decorate a note by adding a melodic twirl in the middle, as shown in either of the two possibilities, *left*. Whichever you choose, the rhythm and velocities should be smooth enough not to break the flow of the melodic line.

Written as:

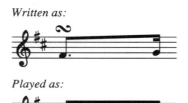

Played as:

Or:

Precision of note-lengths is paramount in classical music – notes covered by curved lines (slurs) should sound completely *legato* although the last note within a slur is usually shortened somewhat. Notes marked with *staccato* dots may be anything from 10-90% of their written length, depending on what sounds good and which voice you are using.

Some suggestions for fingering have been added in the first half of the piece – these are worth persevering with, as they are designed to get the fingers in the right position for playing *legato*. Getting this right on input will save much time messing around with the mouse when editing note lengths. The numbers assume that you will play the top two staves with the right hand, and the bass stave with the left. Comfortable fingering will vary from one player to another – try your own in the second half, always looking ahead to make sure you have a finger ready to play the next note.

By this time, composers were starting to add performance directions to their music. These were not always complete, however, and editors often make good any obvious omissions by using dotted slurs or marks within brackets. The directions *mancando* (getting softer) and *dolce* (sweetly) show Mozart clearly writing for the piano, whose potential for tonal variety was by now ousting the harpsichord in popularity. No speed was indicated, however, as players would have known the tempo of a minuet: try a steady 76 bpm.

Minuet in D K. 355 — Mozart

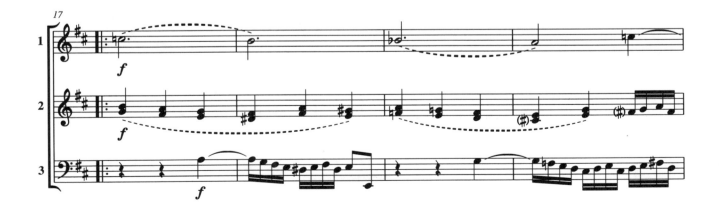

Franz Schubert

The mystery surrounding the causes of Mozart's death in 1791, at the age of 35, together with his quite extraordinary fluency and output as a composer, has provided fuel for discussion (and the odd conspiracy theory) ever since. Schubert's working life was even shorter. He died of syphilis in 1828 at 31, yet a legacy of over 600 songs and a vast amount of other music suggests he was something of a workaholic. Despite such effort, much of Schubert's music was virtually unknown outside his immediate circle and his melodic and harmonic genius was not fully appreciated until many decades after his death.

This *Moment Musicale,* with its fashionably French title, is a perfect example of the evocative and relatively easy piano piece which was in demand by the growing amateur market of the 1820s.

NOTATION

The small notes with lines through the tail are known as **acciaccaturas** ("crushed notes"), and are normally played simultaneously with the main note but given the shortest possible length. Here, however, all the ornaments will feature better if played as thirty-second notes immediately *before* the beat. It will probably be simplest to do your main quantizing before adding them.

The sign over the final chord indicates a **pause**, which means that the note lengths could spill over into a new bar. The *staccato* dots in the first two bars are clearly intended to apply to the whole of the left hand part even though they are not printed throughout. Another convention of printed music offsets any adjacent notes in chords to make them easier to read (as in bar 9). These should, of course, be played simultaneously with the rest of the chord. Notes marked with an accent sign (>) should sound slightly louder than the others.

Allegro moderato (86 - 100 bpm)

Notice that bars 51 - 58 can be copied from bars 3 - 10.

DYNAMICS

ppp	*Extremely soft*
pp	*Very soft*
p	*Soft*
f	*Loud*
dim	*Getting softer*
$\diagdown$	*Getting softer*
$\diagup$	*Getting louder*

One of the most pervasive sounds in urban Vienna would have been the regular beat of horse's hooves on cobbled streets, a rhythm that seems to be suggested by the constant eighth-note pulse of this piece. Some performers take the analogy still further by interpreting Schubert's few dynamic markings *(see left)* as a gradual soft-loud-soft arch throughout the piece to suggest the passing of a carriage on one of the leafy boulevards. In any case, some extended grading of velocities may be rewarding, along with a broad *rit.* (slowing down) in the concluding bars.

The original music was in F minor, a semitone higher than printed here. Transpose the piece back up if you wish, although E minor is probably closer to the pitch that Schubert would have heard.

VOICING

Readers who are not afraid of accusations of bad taste will seize the chance to orchestrate this piano piece. Possibilities include adding a percussion part (**tambourine**, **wood-block** or even **sleigh bells**) with a variety of melodic voices to contrast the various eight-bar sections – we used **muted trumpet** and **marimba**, amongst others. The accompaniment would work well on **electric piano** and duplicate tracks can be created for the loud section, perhaps voiced to **brass**. A separate **bass** part could be made by recording just the first and third eighth-notes of each bar in the lower stave onto a separate track.

Developments

FURTHER SEQUENCING

With the size of the orchestra and the scale of development of musical ideas increasing throughout the classical period, sequencer users who wish to tackle the major works of the time are faced with some exciting (if lengthy!) sessions at the synth. Here are a few famous and manageable suggestions:

Haydn	Symphony № 94 *(The Surprise)*, second movement
	Trumpet Concerto
	Variations in F minor for piano
Mozart	Serenade for 13 wind instruments, K.361
	Rondo in A minor for piano, K.511
	Papageno's "Magic Bells" aria from *The Magic Flute*
	Rondo alla Turca from Piano Sonata in A, K.331
	Piano Concerto in C, K.467, second movement

With Beethoven there are, for the most part, few miniatures – anything you tackle will be on a grand scale. Anyone who has not attempted a sequenced version of the first movement of his Third *(Eroica)* Symphony hasn't really lived! Also try:

Beethoven	Symphony № 5, fourth movement
	Symphony № 7, second movement
	Symphony № 8, third movement
	Symphony № 9, the big tune from the last movement

Schubert is less well-known for his large scale orchestral works, although the 'Great' C major Symphony (particularly the last movement) will provide one of the longest and most exhilarating sequences imaginable. Other essential Schubert includes:

Schubert	Octet, third movement
	Piano Quintet, *The Trout*, particularly the fourth movement
	An die Musik (song with piano accompaniment)
	Incidental Music to *Rosamunde*
	(a movement from this can be found in *Music in Sequence*)

Sequence 9
Tournedos Rossini

It is impossible not to warm to Gioachino Rossini, the epicurean bon viveur who lent his name to a cardiac nightmare of a dish consisting of fillet steak with artichoke hearts, foie gras, truffles and madeira sauce. Although he lived to the ripe old age of 76, his composing career was scarcely longer than that of Schubert – he simply stopped work in 1829, after a string of hugely successful operas, and retired to eat. Wealthy, good humoured and with a young second wife, Rossini proceeded to indulge himself for a further forty years. He did not break this self-imposed silence until 1863, when he composed a highly operatic mass. Presumably written with an eye to the hereafter, he described the work as the last mortal sin of his old age. The fact that it was now possible for a musician to earn a huge fortune and international fame from his art is further indication of the changing status of music in the nineteenth century.

Overture to The Italian Girl in Algiers

One of the functions of an overture is as an orchestral curtain-raiser to an opera, often giving a foretaste of music to be heard later. Rossini is known to have written many of his overtures at the last possible moment, sometimes only hours before the first performance. When there wasn't even time for this, he simply salvaged an overture from an earlier, forgotten opera. Rossini was famous for featuring long *crescendos,* sometimes disguising music which would otherwise, and in less skilful hands, risk sounding rather repetitive.

The extract printed *overleaf* is the last section of this overture. We have compressed the score onto five staves, with suggestions for restoring the feel of the original orchestration. Rossini is always very economical with his material so you will still find many patterns that can be copied.

NOTATION

The wedge shaped marks from bar 25 onwards indicate a heavy *staccato* while the *sf (sforzando)* in bars 58 and 59 requires a much more dramatic accent. All eighth notes can probably be *staccato* from bar 47 onwards. The extra beam across the stems of many notes in Track 4 is shorthand for a *tremolo* – each printed note being played as repeated sixteenths. To save having to play so many repeated chords, you could record bars 37 to 57 using eighth notes throughout. Then make a copy of the section and delay or offset this new part by a sixteenth to alternate with the original eighths.

RECORDING

Record the five staves on Tracks 1 to 5, ignoring the repeat, the grace notes in the last bar of Track 4 and the whole of the percussion part for the moment. It is often easiest to put the bass part (stave 5) down first. Quantize to sixteenths, except in bars 4 and 8 of Track 2, which will need twelfths (8T) resolution. Voice and copy the tracks as follows:

> Program changes can usually be inserted at precise locations within a track to override any initial voice number.

Track 1	**Piccolo**	with temporary program change to **clarinet** in bar 5
Track 2	**Oboe**	with program change to **strings** at bar 25 and back to **oboe** after the first note of bar 29
Track 3	**Horns**	Changing to **trumpet** at bar 41
Track 4	**Strings**	With offset copy of bars 37-57 as explained *above*
Track 5	**Strings**	Using **pizz strings** for the first 8 bars
Track 6	**Bassoon**	Copy of Track 5 from bar 29 to the end
Track 7	**Strings**	Copy of Track 5 transposed down 12 semitones (this also changes from *pizz* to bowed strings at bar 9)
Track 8	**Clarinet**	Copy of Track 2 from second note of bar 29 onwards
Track 9	**Strings**	Copy of Track 1 from second note of bar 29 onwards

The piccolo is a small flute which sounds an octave higher than written – a **flute** will work on this part if transposed up 12 semitones. A mellow brass voice can be used for the start of Track 3, but try to increase the brightness as the music hots up around bar 41. An **acoustic guitar** can substitute for the *pizz* strings on Track 5. If you use **electric bass** in bars 1 to 8 of Track 7, it is unlikely that this section will need to be transposed down an octave.

Make a copy of bars 1 to 12 and insert this at bar 13 to form the repeat, and add the grace notes just *before* the first beat of the last bar. The dynamics suggest a steady *crescendo* from bars 25 to 47. Velocity editing will help to make this even, and the effect may be intensified in the final performance by subtle boosting of the synth's volume control.

TIP You can give the music added excitement by increasing the tempo a few bpm at key points in the score (e.g. bars 37 and 47). Orchestral conductors use this trick to take account of the fact that a completely regular fast tempo can seem to lose its impetus after a while.

PERCUSSION TRACK

Untuned percussion instruments became popular in nineteenth century music, particularly those known as "Turkish" percussion – cymbals, triangle and bass drum. Rossini provides only an outline of the part, using note tails up for the triangle and down for the bass drum. From bar 47 all three instruments presumably play the same part.

Generating the sound of two cymbals crashing together is difficult on synths without orchestral percussion voices, as the crash cymbal in a drum kit is only a single cymbal hit with a stick. If you can't obtain or program a specifically orchestral cymbal voice, try using a loud combination of crash, ride and open hi-hat cymbals, together with as many other metallic sounds as you can spare.

A kit bass drum also has little of the deep resonance of the five-foot orchestral version – a very low **timp** note may be nearer the mark.

TIP Substitutes for a triangle are easier to find – a very high **glock** should do the trick. Two simultaneous notes six semitones apart will help to produce the diffuse range of overtones needed.

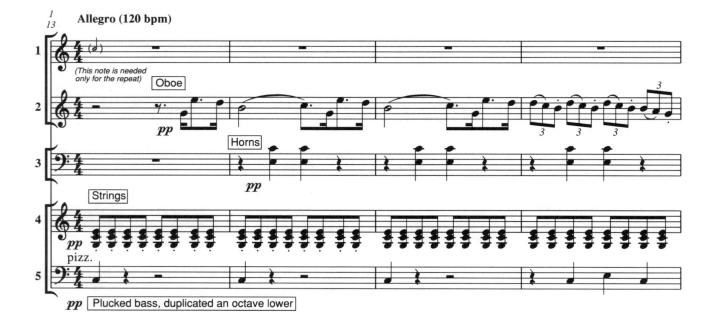

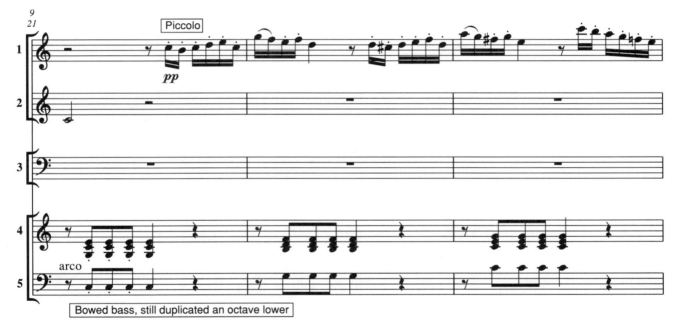

Bowed bass, still duplicated an octave lower

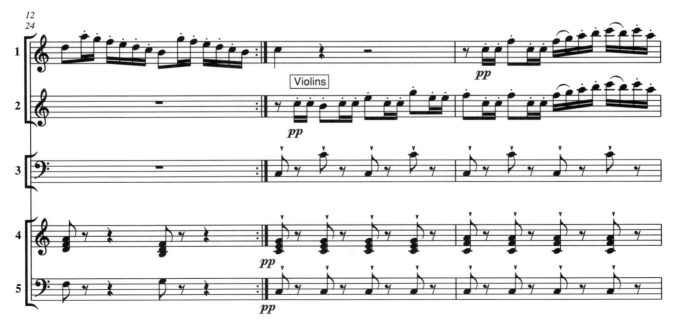

Tournedos Rossini

Fact Sheet
Orchestral Scores

*Realistic sequencing of orchestral music is virtually impossible without the use of a score which shows the exact part played by each instrument. The full scores used by conductors are elusive and expensive, but small versions, known as miniature scores, are available from most music stores and provide a valuable sequencing resource. The score is generally laid out as follows, although not all of these instruments will appear in every piece. All staves that are meant to sound simultaneously will be linked into a **system** with a vertical line at the left of the page. Each stave will usually be labelled with its instrument, although abbreviations are often used after the first page. When instruments are silent for a complete line, their staves will often be omitted to save space. Some parts are not written at their sounding pitch and will need to be transposed – despite every appearance to the contrary, all the pitched instruments are actually sounding a note F in the example below:*

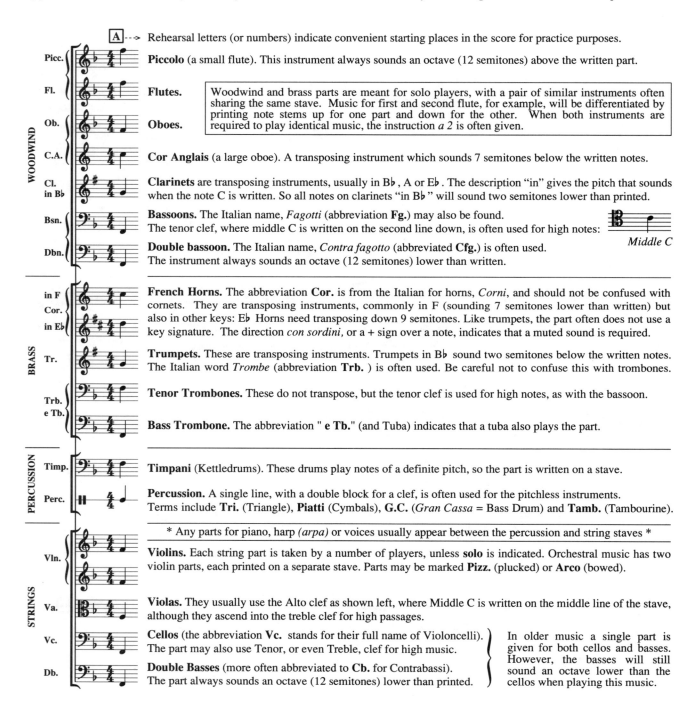

A --> Rehearsal letters (or numbers) indicate convenient starting places in the score for practice purposes.

Piccolo (a small flute). This instrument always sounds an octave (12 semitones) above the written part.

Flutes.

Oboes.

> Woodwind and brass parts are meant for solo players, with a pair of similar instruments often sharing the same stave. Music for first and second flute, for example, will be differentiated by printing note stems up for one part and down for the other. When both instruments are required to play identical music, the instruction *a 2* is often given.

Cor Anglais (a large oboe). A transposing instrument which sounds 7 semitones below the written notes.

Clarinets are transposing instruments, usually in B♭, A or E♭. The description "in" gives the pitch that sounds when the note C is written. So all notes on clarinets "in B♭" will sound two semitones lower than printed.

Bassoons. The Italian name, *Fagotti* (abbreviation **Fg.**) may also be found.
The tenor clef, where middle C is written on the second line down, is often used for high notes:

Middle C

Double bassoon. The Italian name, *Contra fagotto* (abbreviated **Cfg.**) is often used.
The instrument always sounds an octave (12 semitones) lower than written.

French Horns. The abbreviation **Cor.** is from the Italian for horns, *Corni*, and should not be confused with cornets. They are transposing instruments, commonly in F (sounding 7 semitones lower than written) but also in other keys: E♭ Horns need transposing down 9 semitones. Like trumpets, the part often does not use a key signature. The direction *con sordini,* or a + sign over a note, indicates that a muted sound is required.

Trumpets. These are transposing instruments. Trumpets in B♭ sound two semitones below the written notes. The Italian word *Trombe* (abbreviation **Trb.**) is often used. Be careful not to confuse this with trombones.

Tenor Trombones. These do not transpose, but the tenor clef is used for high notes, as with the bassoon.

Bass Trombone. The abbreviation " **e Tb.**" (and Tuba) indicates that a tuba also plays the part.

Timpani (Kettledrums). These drums play notes of a definite pitch, so the part is written on a stave.

Percussion. A single line, with a double block for a clef, is often used for the pitchless instruments.
Terms include **Tri.** (Triangle), **Piatti** (Cymbals), **G.C.** (*Gran Cassa* = Bass Drum) and **Tamb.** (Tambourine).

> * Any parts for piano, harp *(arpa)* or voices usually appear between the percussion and string staves *

Violins. Each string part is taken by a number of players, unless **solo** is indicated. Orchestral music has two violin parts, each printed on a separate stave. Parts may be marked **Pizz.** (plucked) or **Arco** (bowed).

Violas. They usually use the Alto clef as shown left, where Middle C is written on the middle line of the stave, although they ascend into the treble clef for high passages.

Cellos (the abbreviation **Vc.** stands for their full name of Violoncelli). The part may also use Tenor, or even Treble, clef for high music.

Double Basses (more often abbreviated to **Cb.** for Contrabassi). The part always sounds an octave (12 semitones) lower than printed.

In older music a single part is given for both cellos and basses. However, the basses will still sound an octave lower than the cellos when playing this music.

Sequence 10
Clogs and Pumps

Rossini's operas were not the only events pulling the crowds into European opera houses at this time. French composers had long shown an interest in the theatrical possibilities of dance, and the ballet was by now established as an indispensable part of most operas as well as being an entertainment in its own right. Rossini himself was attracted to Paris where his final opera, William Tell, was produced. His young French chorus master at the Paris Opéra, Ferdinand Hérold, was one of many minor composers unable to shake off Rossini's all-pervasive influence. Hérold's ballet score La Fille Mal Gardée (1828) is a compilation of anonymous earlier dances and borrowings from other composers, as well as a substantial amount of original music. It is now best known in a modern version by John Lanchbery, made in 1960 for the Royal Ballet, Covent Garden, on which the arrangement of this first sequence is based.

Clog Dance

We have printed the score in $\frac{4}{4}$ time, although it has a strong triplet feel with the beats in many parts being divided into threes. Sections which need no such subdivision, such as the whole of stave 9, have been printed in straight eighths or quarters for clarity. However, these can safely be included in the necessary triplet quantization.

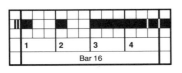

Quantizing to 12ths (8T) will work for all tracks up to bar 25, although 24ths (16T) will be needed for the very short upbeats in the oboe and clarinet parts from bar 26 onwards, and in the wood block solo at bar 33. Grace notes should sound before the beat and, as always, should be inserted after any quantization has been done. The grids shown *left* may help to interpret the difficult oboe rhythms in bars 16 and 27. It is important to realize that notes within triplets last for only two-thirds of their normal length – setting the sequencer's grid resolution for triplets, as shown here, will help to clarify alignment.

TIP There are several pauses in the Introduction. The first of these prolongs the clarinet note in bar 5 while the others lengthen the rests. To get the right effect you can either temporarily reduce the tempo on these beats or, more likely, you will have to change the time signature to 6/4 or even more in the pause bars to gain the necessary space.

MIDI VOLUME CONTROLLER

This piece includes *crescendos* and *diminuendos* not only through patterns of notes but also on single notes. The latter can only be made using MIDI **Volume Controller** (Controller 7). The necessary data can be recorded automatically as MIDI information if you use a foot swell pedal assigned to Volume Controller (manipulating the synth's volume control will not do the trick!) otherwise it will need to be inserted into the track by hand. A large number of values will be needed for a *crescendo* to sound smooth – sequencers with graphic editors will prove very much quicker for this type of task (see *left*).

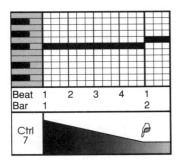

Making a diminuendo on the first note by shaping MIDI Controller 7 data with a graphic editor.

The voicing of the sequence should be clear from the score. The *8va* sign above the flute stave in bars 19-26 indicates that this part should be transposed up an octave. The wind parts are otherwise printed at pitch in this version and do not need transposing. There is also no need for the string bass to be moved down an octave in this sequence. The brass parts are mostly on horns, but notice the changes to trumpet later. We have simplified John Lanchbery's scoring a little: a worthwhile extra would be to duplicate staves 2 and 3 on strings in bars 19-25 and their repeat.

Clog Dance *from* La Fille Mal Gardeé   Hérold / Lanchbery

Moderato con moto (♩ = 110 bpm)

Les Ballets Russes

The craze for ballet soon, like most things French, spread to Russia – the famous Bol'shoy Theatre being built in 1825. Russian composers were quick to establish a distinctive national voice, with a special flair for sparkling orchestration and folk-influenced melody. The vivid colours and rhythms of romantic Russian music were ideally suited to the limelight theatricality of the ballet and produced some of its most memorable scores.

The next two extracts give the opportunity to use instrumental timbres which are seldom given such prominent parts in orchestral music. The cor anglais (a low oboe), harp and bass clarinet had found a place in the expanded orchestras of early 19th-century French opera, while the celeste (a keyboard instrument with metal bars struck by hammers) was invented in 1886.

The silvery tone quality of the celeste fired the imagination of Tchaikovsky, who heard this new instrument in Paris and incorporated it into his ballet score, The Nutcracker (1892). We have included just the first part of the "Dance of the Sugar Plum Fairy" here, although another movement from the ballet can be found in *Music in Sequence*.

The celeste part can be voiced for **glock**, although **vibes** or even **electric piano** would do. Notice that the upper stave should sound an octave higher than written throughout – none of the other music needs transposing. A soft, low **sax** could be substituted for bass clarinet.

Staves 1 and 2 have been omitted at the start of the piece as these instruments don't come in until later. Notice that bars 13-16, with the exception of stave 2, are a copy of bars 5-8: efficiency experts will spot other time-saving copies.

Danse de la Fée-Dragée

Prince Igor

The music *opposite* is the opening section of the Polovtsian Dances, a ballet sequence from Borodin's opera Prince Igor, written in 1870. The music on stave 1 needs distinctive solo voices, but the parts on staves 2 and 3 are a composite version of the original supporting woodwind lines and it may be worth experimenting with the voicing of these to get good blend and balance. The term *dolce* (sweetly) indicates the mood required for this backing.

ARPEGGIATION

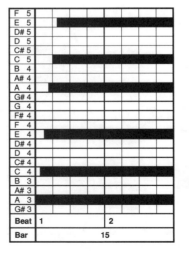

We have printed the harp part on a single stave to clarify the shape of the *arpeggios* – quickly spread chords indicated by the wavy lines in bar 15. All the following harp chords should be treated in the same way. Some sequencers offer an arpeggiation function for chords, otherwise you will have to stagger the note starts as shown *left*.

Stave 6 is for *pizzicato* cellos throughout, so there is no need to make an octave copy for basses. The other (bowed) strings are not needed until bar 14, so stave 5 is omitted at the beginning. Their initial high chord is marked with a small circle in the original score, requiring live players to use harmonics – lightly stopping the string to produce a very soft, flute-like effect.

TIP Care will be needed if quantizing stave 1 on the first page as it contains both sixteenth notes and twelfths (8T). When both triplet and normal values are present in the same part, any quantization of the *whole* section will have to be to the lowest common denominator – the smallest value that is divisible by all of the note-lengths involved. Here, quantization to 48ths (32T) is needed, 48 being divisible by both 16 and 12. However, such a fine quantize value may not shift all notes sufficiently so it may be easier (and musically more expressive) to play the music in freehand.

Borodin wrote the score in A major – transposing the music up two semitones from the simpler key of G printed here will restore the flavour of the original.

Polovtsian Dances *from* Prince Igor

FURTHER SEQUENCING

Rossini	*La Gazza Ladra* and *William Tell* overtures
Mendelssohn	Incidental music to *A Midsummer Night's Dream*
	Hebrides Overture ("Fingal's Cave")
Berlioz	*Roman Carnival* overture
	March to the Scaffold from *Symphonie Fantastique*
Gounod	Ballet Music from *Faust*
	Ave Maria (based on a Prelude in C major by Bach)
Verdi	Grand March and Ballet Music from the opera *Aïda*
Delibes	Mazurka and *Waltz of the Hours* from the ballet *Coppélia*
Bizet	*L'Arlésienne* and *Carmen* Suites
	Au fond du temple saint (duet from *The Pearl Fishers*)
Mussorgsky	*Pictures at an Exhibition* (piano or orchestrated by Ravel)
Grieg	*In the Hall of the Mountain King* from the *Peer Gynt* Suite
Ponchielli	*Dance of the Hours* from the opera *La Gioconda*
Offenbach	"Can-can" from the operetta *Orpheus in the Underworld*
Tchaikovsky	*Dance of the Swans* from the ballet *Swan Lake*
Dvorak	Slow movement of Symphony № 9 (*New World*)

Connoisseurs of romantic music will notice that our selection of nineteenth century composers omits many other famous names: Schumann, Chopin, Liszt, Brahms, Wagner ... there is a wealth of music to draw upon from this period.

Fact Sheet
Effects

*The term **effects** covers a number of ways of processing an audio signal to enhance the raw sound. In pop music a wide variety of effects are used creatively to modify and sometimes even completely distort the source material, but in classical music effects are added more subtly and in order to make the final product sound as realistic as possible.*

EFFECTS UNITS

Effects can be applied either to the entire output of a synth or to individual tracks via a mixing desk. Separate units are available for each different type of effect required, but a **multi effects processor** is often enough for the small studio, offering a selection of programs. More elaborate models will allow the use of two or more effects at the same time and often include a MIDI interface so that settings can be made and changed to suit individual pieces from a track of control messages on the sequencer.

Synth workstations often have on-board effects units, although these will generally only operate on the synth's own voices and will therefore be of no help if you want to include other sound sources or live tracks in your final mix. For sequencing purposes it is probably best to apply your main effects to the multi-timbral combination as a whole, unless you want an ensemble of instruments that sound as if they are all playing in different rooms.

Despite the variety and complexity of effects provided by keenly competing manufacturers, studio engineers with an eye to getting the job done concern themselves principally with equalization and reverberation. Indeed, of all the effects available, reverb is the most useful as it allows you to create the impression of placing your music in a particular setting, be it a concert hall, a small studio, or even a broom cupboard if you wish.

REVERBERATION

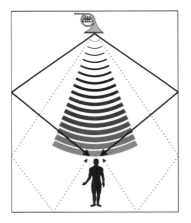

Direct sound (the curved lines) reaches the listener first, followed by Early Reflections from nearby surfaces (the solid lines). Finally, diffuse multiple reflections (shown by the dotted lines) add a sheen of reverberation to the original sound.

Reverberation results from the way sound waves are reflected around the hard surfaces of a hall or room. These reflected waves have longer to travel and therefore arrive at the ear later and less powerfully than the direct waves, effectively prolonging the original sound. This is not quite the same as an **echo** which is strictly a sound reflected back with such delay and force that it appears quite separate from the original – as when shouting across a canyon.

In a large hall, a reverb time of about 2 seconds is ideal for classical music, overlapping and blending different sounds without confusing them. Longer times of 6 seconds or more occur in very large buildings like cathedrals, but these pose real problems for fast, loud music which inextricably merges together. Music that is awash in a sea of reverb loses all detail and precision and is too often a sign of the amateur engineer hoping to paper over the cracks in an untidy mix.

Reverberation times shorter than 2 seconds aid the clarity of speech, but are disliked by musicians as they make the music sound dead and exposed, leaving any tiny gaps and inconsistencies clearly audible. However, it is common for commercial music to be recorded in dry studio conditions so that "takes" can be edited together without the problems caused by natural reverb spilling over into adjacent parts or tracks. Electronic reverb is then added at a later stage in the process to add a realistic sheen to the end product.

The most noticeable thing about reverb is its length. The reverb time should be decided by *where* you wish your listener to imagine the performance is taking place. Effects units provide a large selection of "room sizes" – church, large hall, small hall, medium room, etc. – each with variable reverb times.

The mix of direct and processed signal is also important. A high proportion of direct sound will put the listener near the front of the hall, but may require a large ensemble to be well panned out in the stereo field if an artificial, "tunnel" effect is to be avoided. Too little direct sound will give the impression of being at the back of a 500 metre stadium.

Early reflections settings enable you to simulate the effect of sitting close to a wall where the reverberations merge less well. The short wave lengths of high frequencies are easily absorbed in well furnished halls with drapes and cushions, so decreasing brightness (or high frequency) settings will give the impression of a warm, dark acoustic. Increase it too much, though, and you will place your music amid the glass and concrete of a shopping mall!

EQUALIZATION

Equalization (EQ) is another name for tone controls. The term originally referred to circuits merely for ironing out uneven response in recording equipment, although today few classical sound engineers can resist adding a little extra brightness to simulate the excitement of a live performance.

EQ is a facility normally provided on mixing desks, where it can be applied to each track separately. However, most effects units also include at least a simple two-band equalizer, allowing the levels of high (treble) and low (bass) frequencies to be adjusted to match the response characteristics of your monitor speakers and room. EQ can also be used to filter out undesirable electrical noise such as low frequency mains hum.

Boosting the low frequencies of a weak bass part may simply make it sound boomy and ultimately risk damaging small speakers. However, a three-band equalizer will allow you to bolster the middle range, emphasising the part's overtones to improve the focus. **Graphic equalizers** carry this idea a stage further, offering a number of separately controlled bands across the frequency range. Other forms of EQ include sweep and parametric, both giving fine control over the entire spectrum.

OTHER EFFECTS

Limiters cut back the volume of any exceptionally loud signal, primarily to protect your equipment! **Compressors** go even further, reducing the overall dynamic range so that nothing seems too soft or too loud. Compression is very widely used in broadcasting and commercial recording, largely to funnel the wide dynamic range of live music into a band narrow enough for the signal not to be distorted by low grade equipment or lost in ever increasing levels of background noise. Compression can help to smooth out any irregularities in a singer's voice but it will also remove most of the vivid contrasts that are so much a part of classical music.

Whereas equalization can only boost or cut what is already present, **exciters** or **enhancers** generate extra high frequencies from the data fed through them, adding "presence" to the mix. **Chorusing** fractionally delays and shifts the pitch of a signal: the result, when mixed with the original, can make a thin sound seem more like a group of players, particularly with vocal, string and brass voices on the synth.

Effects units invariably contain a good selection of other effects, including overdrive, fuzz, tremolo, flanging, phasing, delay and pitch shift. Many of these are primarily for processing electric guitar sounds, although you may wish to experiment with them especially if you are into seriously creative voicing of classical music.

Sequence 11
Organ Voluntary

The pipe organ is one of the oldest musical instruments, probably originating in ancient Greece. The ethereal sound of the instrument made it particularly suitable for church services, and the organ became a common fixture in large churches from medieval times onwards. By the 17th century, North German organ builders were producing instruments with a large number of different timbres (called stops) which could be selected and mixed together. These instruments used hundreds of pipes, ranging from thirty-two feet to less than an inch in length. The very low pitches generated by the longest pipes were played with the feet using a pedalboard, while two or more keyboards (manuals) gave access to the ranks of shorter pipes. This was the instrument that inspired Bach, an example of whose organ music appears later in this chapter.

French Organ Music

The organ was less appealing to the generations after Bach, the lack of subtle dynamic control limiting the degree of expression which later composers and audiences demanded. However, a range of 19th century improvements did much to restore its popularity. Among these was the refinement of the swell box – an enclosed section of the organ, with shutters that could be moved by a pedal to produce *crescendos* and *diminuendos*.

Widor's famous Toccata was written in Paris about 1880. The following extract makes good use of the swell pedal, fading to almost nothing between bars 47 and 59 before building once more to the ear-shattering ending. Organ voices (like the real thing) are not generally velocity sensitive so these changes will almost certainly need to be made using MIDI Controller 7, either via a volume pedal or written into the sequencer tracks.

Synth **pipe organ** voices are generally a composite of sounds at different octaves representing a range of stops that an organist might use playing at mid-volume, together with a fair helping of reverb. Here the *fff* indicates "as loud as possible" – really grand organ music like this will need reinforcement from other voices, especially at the bottom end.

In addition to the two staves found in most keyboard music, organists have to get used to a third stave for the pedal part which in Widor's Toccata enters *maestoso* (majestically) at bar 17. This will particularly benefit from being copied down an octave and voiced for the loudest brass. The end of the piece will take everything you can throw at it!

TIP If you have more than one pipe organ voice available, try doubling up all the tracks, panning them left and right, since organs produce a very wide spectrum of sounds. However, note that voices simply labelled **organ** are likely to reproduce the very different sound of an electric organ.

Rock versions have been made of both of the pieces in this chapter. A solid organ sound will still be needed as a foundation, with sections on harpsichord and electric piano, perhaps punctuated by atmospheric swirls based on the underlying chord pattern. Heavy bass voices on the pedal part will give the music drive, as will a fast rock drum pattern, perhaps also starting at bar 17.

The constant sixteenth notes in the top stave make this part ideal for step writing. All the sections beginning with an *8va* sign need to be transposed up an octave. The instruction *loco* ("in its place") indicates untransposed music.

Allegro (100 bpm)

8va - - - - - - - - - - - - - - -

fff

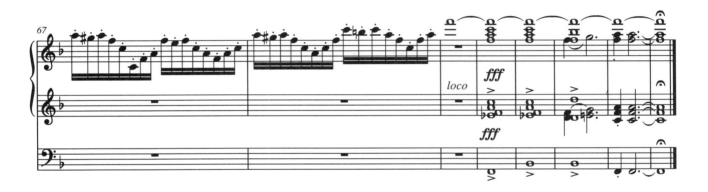

Back to Bach

By the nineteenth century, a taste for performing music from earlier periods was already starting to appear, especially with the rediscovery of Bach's music. His Toccata in D minor (pre-1708) is perhaps the most famous organ piece of all. Its improvisatory style and frequent pauses pose a challenge to the sequencer user who wants to fit the music into a regular metronome beat.

The most musical solution for a skilled player would be to switch off the metronome and record the piece freehand. However, this is by no means easy so we have printed above the original notation an alternative version of the two most awkward sections. This will allow you to keep to a regular beat while still achieving a reasonably free interpretation of the ornaments, arpeggiation and pauses. Notice that these alternatives add three bars to the original length – the printed bar numbers take this into account.

The little slurs on the small staves in bars 4 and 13 indicate that each note should be sustained until the end of the arpeggio. Bars 15 to 18 on the middle stave might be easier to record as straight sixteenths: the pattern can then be shifted later by one thirty-second note into its correct position. The tempo indications are ours and give only an outline of the variety of pace which players traditionally use in this piece. As with the Widor, rich voicing will add much to the texture, especially on the pedal part.

Toccata in D Minor

J. S. Bach

(45 bpm)

(72 bpm)

Sequence 12
Birds and Bees

Short pieces of music designed to evoke the mood and character of a particular event or scene became hugely popular in the nineteenth century. The upholstered piano stools in countless drawing rooms were crammed to overflowing with songs and pieces under titles such as "From Long Ago" or "To A Wild Rose", as well as arrangements of popular hits from orchestral music and opera. The two famous pieces in this chapter have been published in versions for every conceivable instrument, with the obligatory piano accompaniment. It may reassure you to realize that not even the most far-out synth voicing can compete for weirdness with the red-faced spectacle of an amateur tuba player attempting the Flight of the Bumble Bee.

The Carnival of the Animals

Saint-Saëns wrote *The Carnival of the Animals* in 1886 as an entertainment for his friends. Worried that his reputation as a pillar of the French musical establishment might suffer, he banned further performances of all but the following movement until after his death in 1921. "The Swan" was written for solo cello and two pianos, although the second piano part is so minimal that it is omitted here.

MIDI SUSTAIN CONTROLLER

You will notice that the accompaniment throughout simply outlines the chords – pianists would use the sustaining pedal to keep all of the notes of a pattern sounding until the chord changes, *eg* at bars 3 and 5. Even if your synth does not have a sustaining pedal, it will probably be able to respond to MIDI Sustain Pedal messages (Controller 64) written into the sequencer track. Don't forget to reset to zero at the end of every chord pattern. Another way to enhance the smoothness of this accompaniment would be to produce an extra track of straight chords, using a quiet sustaining voice.

The solo line needs to be as expressive as possible. The slurs printed in string music generally show groups of notes to be played within one stroke of the bow rather than real phrasing. However, the instruction *sempre* (always) *legato* indicates that the music should be played smoothly throughout.

Cellists use a wide range of dynamics and vibrato in this piece, especially on the long notes (the higher the note, the faster the vibrato). The music will sound best if it is not heavily quantized – only the first note of each bar needs to co-ordinate precisely with the accompaniment. String players might also use a technique known as *portamento* in this style of music, sliding at the last moment to the pitch of the next note rather than hitting it cleanly. A few synths implement *portamento* as a device that can be used on the keyboard.

Try a slow tempo of 54–60 bpm: the term *lento* in bar 25 suggestions a still slower speed at this point. The instruction *15ma* in the following bar indicates that this passage should sound two octaves higher than written. We have printed the whole movement five semitones higher than its original key – transposition back down will suit the range of the cello, although the solo part does not necessarily have to be on a string voice at all. We produced an attractive version on **ping wave** with **vibes** accompaniment; for once, a really slow-speaking voice can be a positive advantage!

The Swan *from* The Carnival of the Animals — Saint-Saëns

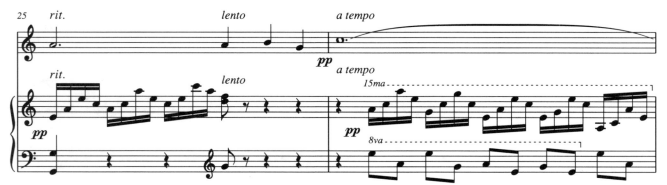

This piece first appeared in 1900 as an orchestral-cum-vocal interlude in Rimsky-Korsakoff's opera *The Legend of Tsar Saltan,* although the original has since been eclipsed by numerous arrangements for solo instrument and piano. The abbreviated version here takes advantage of the wide pitch range of the synth – although you will have to transpose the beginning and ending after input if your keyboard spans only four octaves.

Apart from the five bar intro, which should sound suitably rousing, the accompaniment could use **pizz strings** or **guitar**, especially if contrasted with a brass or woodwind voice on the solo (try **trumpet** or **flute**). The important changes in dynamics in bars 9-12 plus some wildly creative panning will help give the impression of an angry bee in flight. The tempo (originally 144 bpm) can be as fast as is believable – 200 bpm is about the limit!

The sequence has two repeated sections and can be constructed as follows:
   Record bars 1 to 40, ending with the first time bar.
   Copy bars 29 to 39 to fill bars 41 to 51.
   Record bars 52 (the second time bar) to 60 (another first time bar).
   Copy from the sign at bar 9 to bar 59 to fill bars 61 to 111.
   Finally, record bars 112 (the second time bar) to the end.

The Flight of the Bumble Bee   Rimsky-Korsakoff

Birds and Bees

Developments

FURTHER SEQUENCING

Some other popular instrumental solos (all for piano unless shown otherwise) that should sequence well include:

Chopin	*Minute* Waltz (Opus 64, Nº 1)
	Revolutionary Étude (Opus 10, Nº 12)
Liszt	Hungarian Rhapsody Nº 2
	Liebesträume Nº 3
Dvorak	Humoresque (Opus 101, Nº 7)
Godard	Valse for flute and piano (from Opus 116)
Fauré	Elégie for cello and piano (Opus 24)
	Sicilienne for violin and piano (Opus 78)
Saint-Saëns	Other movements from *The Carnival of the Animals* especially "Fossils" featuring a xylophone solo
Elgar	*Salut d'Amour* (Opus 12)
	Chanson de Matin for violin and piano (Opus 15)
	Chanson de Nuit for violin and piano (Opus 15)
MacDowell	*To a Wild Rose*
Koenig	*Post Horn Galop* for brass
Arban	Variations on *Carnival of Venice* for trumpet and piano
Greenwood	*The Acrobat* for trombone and piano

Sequence 13
French Impressions

With benefit of hindsight it is often possible to identify certain moments as being turning points in the development of the arts. These explosions of activity usually seem to occur at the end of periods of stability, for example, London in the time of Shakespeare; Vienna at the end of the 18th century and again around 1910; Liverpool in the early 1960s. A similar ferment of cultural life was happening in Paris in the 1890s, where young poets, painters, musicians and writers gathered nightly at the Chat Noir in Montmartre to debate revolution. Amongst them were two composers who, in their very different ways, were to have a profound effect on the music of the 20th century, Erik Satie and Claude Debussy.

Erik Satie

Satie was a true eccentric. Much involved in the avant-garde theatre of the time, he was always interested in challenging the traditional orthodoxies. He gave his music surreal titles, such as the *Three Pieces in the form of a Pear,* and explored new soundscapes by including parts for typewriter, siren and revolver in his ballet *Parade*. His experiments included writing music for performance while the audience talked, calling for 840 repetitions of the appropriately named *Vexations,* and dispensing with barlines in some pieces.

The startlingly spare texture of the *Gymnopédies* (1888) for piano is the antithesis of the lush, overblown style of romanticism which Satie and his contemporaries felt was strangling music at this time.

The made-up title hints at the balletic exercises of young athletes in ancient Greece. Aim for a cool, almost hypnotic style when recording and voicing this piece. We have expanded the original notation from two staves to three, but otherwise have made no changes – Satie really does finish like this! The initial marking "Slow and sadly" suggests a tempo of around 82 bpm, and you will need to sustain the harmony through each bar, especially if using a piano voice.

Gymnopédie Nº 1   Satie

Further detail on the daily life of this remarkable composer may be gleaned from the following extract from Satie's own *Memoirs of an Amnesiac:*

An artist must organize his life. Here is my daily timetable. I rise at 7.18; am inspired from 10.23 to 11.47. I lunch at 12.11 and leave the table at 12.14. A healthy ride on horseback round my estate follows from 13.19 to 14.53. More inspiration from 15.12 to 16.07. Various occupations (fencing, reflection, immobility, visits, contemplation, dexterity, water sports, etc.) between 16.21 and 18.47. Dinner is served at 19.16 and finished at 19.20. I read symphonies out loud from 20.09 to 21.59 and go to bed regularly at 22.37. Once a week (on Tuesdays) I wake with a start at 3.14.

I only eat food that is white: eggs, sugar, shredded bones, the fat of dead animals, veal, salt, coconuts, chicken cooked in white water, mouldy fruit, rice, turnips, sausages in camphor, pastry, cheese (white varieties), cotton salad and certain kinds of fish (without their skin). I boil my wine and drink it cold mixed with Fuchsia juice.

I have a good appetite but never talk when eating for fear of strangling myself. I breathe carefully (a little at a time). I very rarely dance. When walking I hold my ribs and look steadily behind me. My expression is very serious: if I laugh it is unintentional and I always apologize politely. I sleep very soundly with one eye closed. My bed is round with a hole in it for my head to go through. Every hour a servant takes my temperature and gives me another. For a long time I have subscribed to a fashion magazine. I wear a white cap, white socks and a white waistcoat. My doctor has always told me to smoke otherwise, as he says, someone else will smoke instead.

The Pipes of Pan

While Satie's experimentations led him into areas which ranged from the odd to the downright surreal, Debussy was far more influential on subsequent composers with his impressionistic approach to musical colour. His interests encompassed the use of new scales (such the whole tone scale at the end of this piece) and the newly discovered sound world of the Indonesian Gamelan.

Syrinx is the name for the pipes played by the god Pan in Greek mythology. Their hollow, breathy quality is reproduced well by synth **pan flute** *voices.*

This solo flute piece, originally a semitone higher than printed here, was written in 1913 for the play *Psyche*. Debussy included no bar lines, phrasing or tempo markings, although we have suggested some ideas. It is impossible to convey the wistful mood if you play strictly in time with the metronome. Since there are no additional tracks to align, you can switch the beep off and go for an improvisatory feel, using the sequencer as a simple tape recorder. The group of five notes in bar 34 should take up the space of two beats, although in this piece many of the rhythms can be interpreted quite freely.

Syrinx — Debussy

Just a little faster

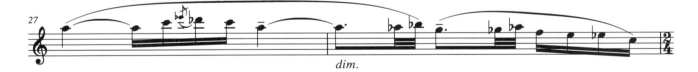

Sequence 14
Finishing Orff

Perhaps the only common factor in twentieth century music is its diversity. Since Debussy, Western composers have felt able to explore new scales, chords, rhythms and instruments in a way that would have been unimaginable even fifty years earlier. Influences from folk, jazz and popular music have been absorbed, along with a willingness to draw from the parallel disciplines of theatre, philosophy and science, as well as from other traditions and cultures around the world. As we write, even basic musical barriers are being eroded, with the concept of "crossover" very much a buzz-word amongst classical and rock audiences eager for fresh experiences. Two of the most notable features of modern music are its acceptance of harmonic dissonance and preoccupation with rhythm. This can be subtle and hypnotic, as in the kaleidoscopic shifting of Steve Reich's Piano Phase, or energetic and brutal, as shown by the constant time signature changes in the Carl Orff piece below. So, power up the synth, put the cat out and really give the neighbours something to complain about!

Carl Orff and Carmina Burana

The *Carmina Burana* is a set of lyrics collected by 13th-century monks, celebrating in explicit detail the joys of feasting, drinking and making love. Some of the poems were set to music in 1937 by Carl Orff, who used a variety of the simplest rhythmic and melodic patterns to make the work accessible to amateur as well as professional performers. The constant repetitions in this Dance, the only purely instrumental movement, make it ideal music for sequencing, although the ingenuity by which the impact and focus of these patterns are shifted means that the music pulsates with energy.

Before recording, you may need to prepare a template for the sequence by entering all the different time signatures into their respective bar numbers. Some sequencers use a mastertrack for this purpose.

Record the four main tracks and copy out the various repeats. Quantize tightly, being careful not to lose the occasional short notes. We have suggested some voicing to reflect Orff's original orchestration, although you may wish to use alternatives in the extensive string sections. Program changes in the track should be left until all copying is completed. Note the seven tempo changes.

PERCUSSION

As well as the Timpani stave there are parts for other percussion instruments in bars 3–4 and from bar 75 to the end. Notice that bass drum and cymbal have alternate eighth notes in this final section and that all three instruments play the last chord (*see* page 66 for some details on orchestral percussion.)

There is some additional voicing in the final section, from bar 75 onwards, which can be done by copying to new tracks, as follows.

Stave 1	Voiced for **flute** and transposed up an octave
Stave 2	Voiced for **clarinet**
Stave 3	Voiced for **bassoon** and transposed down an octave
Stave 4	Voiced for **trombone** or **low brass**

The last three bars of stave 1 can also be doubled on **glock** (or **vibes**) if you have any voices left by this stage.

Dance *from* Carmina Burana

Carl Orff

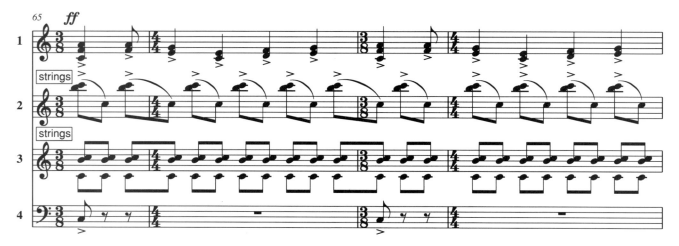

75 **più mosso (146 bpm)**

Minimalist Music

The extract *below* is from one of the earliest pieces of Minimalist music by the American composer Steve Reich. This work grew out of his experiments with the juxtaposition of recorded (fixed) and live (flexible) performances of the same musical material.

Piano Phase, for two pianos (or two marimbas) was written in 1967, and uses identical music in both parts. One player keeps completely strict time while the second player, after a number of synchronized repeats, accelerates very gradually until the two parts are exactly one sixteenth note adrift. The music then stabilizes for between 16 and 24 repeats, after which the process happens again, this time ending two sixteenths apart.

Although we have printed only five bars of music, you can construct much more of the piece by continuing the cycle of acceleration and stabilization ten more times until both parts once again lock onto identical notes.

The initial bar is repeated variable numbers of times, indicated by "x 4-8" (between four and eight repeats). You will ultimately need several hundred copies of this pattern. Track 2 has identical material, fading in at letter B.

Both tracks remain locked together for 12–18 repeats of section B. The dotted stave at letter C represents a section where Track 2 will need to accelerate sufficiently for the rhythms of both tracks to be back in sync by letter D, although the pitches should now be one note out of phase.

The amounts of *accelerando* needed are so tiny that the right effect can be achieved by a single increase in speed at the required points in Track 2, provided you can first **lock** the tempo of Track 1 at 72 bpm. Assuming 10 repeats of the pattern, a new speed of 72.6 bpm will be needed for the phasing sections. Alternatively, a **tempo** or **compex** transform should enable you to compress 121 notes on Track 2 into the time taken by 120 notes (10 bars) on Track 1. We recommend you re-input the Track 2 notes in the first bar of D (and later similar sections) to avoid gaps in the music.

Use the same voice for both parts, setting different MIDI channels to avoid note clipping problems, and pan the tracks left and right. Have fun!

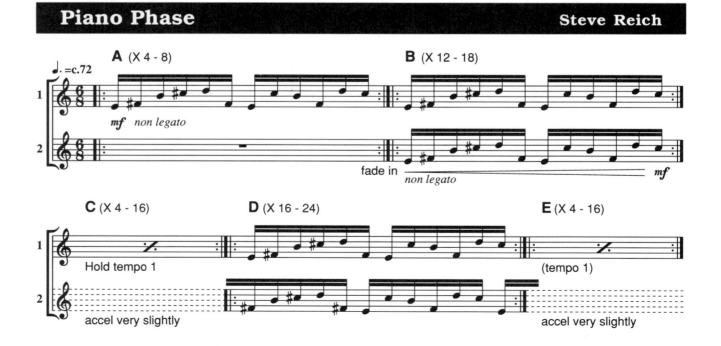

Printed and bound in Great Britain by
Caligraving Limited Thetford Norfolk

9/95 (22354)